PENGUIN  CI

PENGUI͟   ͟S
GENERAL EDITO.   ͟ΌPHER RICKS

SIR GAWAIN AND THE GREEN KNIGHT

Sir Gawain and the Green Knight survives in a single manuscript copy of about 1400, along with three other poems (*Pearl*, *Patience* and *Cleanness*) probably by the same author. His identity is unknown. The dialect of the manuscript points to the north-west of England, and speculation has recently concentrated on the gentry of Cheshire, north-west Staffordshire and south Lancashire – families such as Booth, Mascy, Newton and Stanley – but without as yet arriving at an agreed identification.

J. A. BURROW is Emeritus Professor at the University of Bristol and among the most distinguished English medievalists of his generation. His books include *Ricardian Poetry*, also published by Penguin; *The Ages of Man*; *A Book of Middle English*, with Thorlac Turville-Petre; *Langland's Fictions*; *Thomas Hoccleve*; *Medieval Writers and Their Work*; (ed.) *Thomas Hoccleve's Complaint and Dialogue*; and *The 'Gawain'-Poet*.

Sir Gawain and the Green Knight

EDITED BY J. A. BURROW

PENGUIN BOOKS

PENGUIN BOOKS

Published by the Penguin Group
Penguin Books Ltd, 80 Strand, London WC2R 0RL, England
Penguin Putnam Inc., 375 Hudson Street, New York, New York 10014, USA
Penguin Books Australia Ltd, 250 Camberwell Road, Camberwell, Victoria 3124, Australia
Penguin Books Canada Ltd, 10 Alcorn Avenue, Toronto, Ontario, Canada M4V 3B2
Penguin Books India (P) Ltd, 11 Community Centre, Panchsheel Park, New Delhi – 110 017, India
Penguin Books (NZ) Ltd, Cnr Rosedale and Airborne Roads, Albany, Auckland, New Zealand
Penguin Books (South Africa) (Pty) Ltd, 24 Sturdee Avenue, Rosebank 2196, South Africa

Penguin Books Ltd, Registered Offices: 80 Strand, London WC2R 0RL, England

www.penguin.com

First published 1972
23

Introduction and copyright © J. A. Burrow, 1972
All rights reserved

Printed in Great Britain by Antony Rowe Ltd, Chippenham, Wiltshire
Set in Monotype Ehrhardt

ISBN: 978-0-14-042295-5

Contents

This edition of *Sir Gawain and the Green Knight* rests on the single surviving manuscript copy in the British Museum. All significant departures from the readings of the manuscript are registered in the list on pp. 125–7. The spellings of the scribe have been changed in two ways. Firstly, some obsolete characters and usages have been modernized. Thus, þ becomes *th*; ȝ becomes *gh*, *w*, *y* or *s*, and is occasionally omitted; *w*, where it represents a vowel sound, becomes *u* or *ew*; final *é* becomes *y* or *ee*; and *i/j* and *u/v* are used according to modern practice. Secondly, wherever the scribe spells a word in several different ways, a single spelling has been selected and used in every case, except where rhyme, metre or alliteration require more than one form (e.g. *wothe* 1576, *wathe* 2355, both in rhyme). I have generally chosen the spelling closest to the modern form, where that exists; but I have also tried to show as many distinctions as possible in the spelling of words which might be confused together. Thus, although the scribe spells the verb *hit* in the modern way as well as sometimes writing *hitte*, I have preferred the latter spelling because *hit* is also the form of the neuter pronoun *it*. But distinctions cannot always be established: the definite article and the pronoun *thee* remain confused in my text, because the scribe always spells them both *the*.

The vagaries of the spelling leave many points of pronunciation open to doubt; but the metrical form and expressiveness of the writing will survive even a modern pronunciation. The poet seems not to have sounded final *-e* except occasionally (*sothe* 415 rhymes with *to the*), and there is no question here, as there is in Chaucer's verse, of a delicate metrical organization depending on final *-e*. The rhythms and alliterations of the lines come out quite clearly when the poem is read aloud. Pronounce both the sounds written in the consonant cluster *kn* at the beginning of words: *knight, knokled*.

The inflexions of nouns and verbs also present few practical difficulties. *-s* is the ending for the second as well as the third person singular present indicative of verbs, and also appears in the plural besides the normal *-(e)n* or *-e*: *thou fles, he laghes, thay folwes*. The polite, plural form of the imperative also usually ends in *-s*: *Dos, teches me of your wyt* 1533. The normal ending of the present participle is *-ande* (*-yng* belongs to the verbal noun). Certain unfamiliar pronoun forms are of special importance. *Ho* (sometimes *scho*) means 'she', and *hir* means 'her'. The pronouns of the third person plural are: nominative *thay*, possessive *her* (sometimes *thair*), accusative-dative *hem*. The distinction between *hir* 'her' and *her* 'their' is particularly important. Notice also, in the second person pronouns, the distinction between the plural *ye*, etc., which is polite and formal when a single person is being addressed, and the singular *thou*, etc., which is familiar, or else, where the circumstances do not justify familiarity, insulting (see 258 n, 2140 n).

The syntax is often fluid and informal, and modern conventions of punctuation do not serve it well. (The scribe used no marks of punctuation: all punctuation in the text is editorial, and much of it is open to question.) The following constructions, normal in fourteenth-century English, present difficulties: the use of verbs impersonally without an *it* as subject (*me behoves, as him likes* 'as it pleases him'); the use of adjectives as nouns (*the naked* 'the naked flesh', *the swete* 'the charming lady'); the omission of the relative pronoun when it is the subject of the relative clause (2053); the use of the so-called 'ethic dative' (explained 1905 n); the placing of some prepositions after the nouns they govern (*him by, segges overthwert*); the omission of verbs of motion (2132, 2400). Some difficulties of this sort are treated in the explanatory notes.

The vocabulary of the poem is such as to require quite an extensive glossary. Even words familiar in themselves to modern readers often carry unfamiliar senses. Sometimes this is obvious. No attentive reader could possibly understand *pertly* at 544 or *uncouthe* at 1808 in their modern senses. But other cases are more deceptive. *Fre of his speche* (847) means 'noble [*not* unrestrained] in utterance'; *vilanous* (1497) means 'churlish' *not* 'wicked';

wroth with himselven (1660) means 'angry within [*not* with] himself'; *bounty* (357, 1519) means 'virtue' *not* 'bounty'. Even guileless-looking words such as *chymny* and *somer* (summer) have meanings slightly different from their modern descendants. However, the chief function of the glossary is to explain words which the reader will normally not recognize at all. The poet's north-western dialect contained many expressions (often of Scandinavian origin, e.g. *kay* 'left') which have never had more than regional currency. But the more fundamental cause of lexical difficulty is the sheer copiousness of the poet's diction. Requirements of alliteration explain why he uses a number of synonyms, each beginning with a different sound, for certain simple, recurrent ideas. Words for 'man', besides *mon, knight, lord, prynce*, etc., are: *burn, freke, gome, hathel, lede, renk, schalk, segge* and *wye*. Words for 'horse' are: *blonk, caple, fole, horse, stede*. Often, however, the poet seems to vary his diction just for the love of it, as when Gawain uses the word *mere* 'appointed place' in 1061 and Bertilak uses *merk* in the same sense twelve lines later. The same taste appears in the author's descriptions of hunting, armour, horse-trappings, castle architecture and the like, where technical terminology is very freely used. Those who wish may find all such terms explained briefly in the glossary.

Certain apparent discrepancies may occur between glossary and text over compound words. In such cases the single word in the text has been divided up with a hyphen in the glossary to make the composition of the word clearer.

Acknowledgements

This edition owes a great debt to its predecessors: especially to the edition by J. R. R. Tolkien, E. V. Gordon and N. Davis; but also to that of Sir I. Gollancz, and to those of A. C. Cawley, R. A. Waldron and R. T. Jones. The last-mentioned editor had before I did the idea of regularizing the spelling of the text.

I should like also to acknowledge my indebtedness to Professors Norman Davis and Frank Ll. Harrison, to Mr Ian Robinson and to Mr Thorlac Turville-Petre, for the improvements and corrections which they have suggested to me.

Further Reading

EDITIONS

Sir Gawain and the Green Knight, edited by J. R. R. Tolkien
and E. V. Gordon, second edition revised by Norman Davis,
Oxford University Press, 1967 (hardback and paperback).
The Poems of the Pearl Manuscript, edited by Malcolm Andrew
and Ronald Waldron (York Medieval Texts), Edward Arnold,
1978 (hardback and paperback).
Sir Gawain and the Green Knight, edited and translated by
W. R. J. Barron, Manchester University Press, 1974 (hardback
and paperback).
Sir Gawain and the Green Knight, edited by Theodore
Silverstein, Chicago University Press, 1974 (hardback and
paperback).

VERSE TRANSLATIONS

Sir Gawain and the Green Knight, translated by Brian Stone,
Penguin, 1959 (paperback).
Sir Gawain and the Green Knight, translated by Marie Borroff,
Norton, 1967 paperback).

BOOK-LENGTH STUDIES

David Aers, *Community, Gender and Individual Identity:
English Writing 1360–1430*, Routledge, 1988, pp. 153–78.
L. D. Benson, *Art and Tradition in Sir Gawain and the Green
Knight*, Rutgers University Press, 1965.
Marie Borroff, *Sir Gawain and the Green Knight: A Stylistic
and Metrical Study*, Yale University Press, 1962.

J. A. Burrow, *A Reading of Sir Gawain and the Green Knight*,
Routledge & Kegan Paul, 1965.
W. A. Davenport, *The Art of the Gawain-Poet*, Athlone Press,
1978.
Ad Putter, *Sir Gawain and the Green Knight and French
Arthurian Romance*, Clarendon Press, 1995.
A. C. Spearing, *The Gawain-Poet: A Critical Study*,
Cambridge University Press, 1970.
Sarah Stanbury, *Seeing the Gawain-Poet: Description and
the Act of Perception*, University of Pennsylvania Press,
1991.
E. Wilson, *The Gawain-Poet*, E. J. Brill, 1976.

COLLECTIONS OF CRITICISM

R. J. Blanch (ed.), *Sir Gawain and Pearl: Critical Essays*,
Indiana University Press, 1966 (paperback).
D. Fox (ed.), *Twentieth Century Interpretations of Sir Gawain
and the Green Knight*, Prentice-Hall, 1968 (paperback).
D. R. Howard and C. K. Zacher (eds.), *Critical Studies of Sir
Gawain and the Green Knight*, University of Notre Dame Press,
1968 (hardback and paperback).

CONTEMPORARY BACKGROUND

Michael J. Bennett, *Community, Class and Careerism:
Cheshire and Lancashire Society in the Age of Sir Gawain
and the Green Knight*, Cambridge University Press, 1983.
Maurice Keen, *Chivalry*, Yale University Press, 1984.
Gervase Mathew, *The Court of Richard II*, Murray, 1968.

ARTHURIAN BACKGROUND

R. S. Loomis (ed.), *Arthurian Literature in the Middle Ages*,
Oxford University Press, 1959.
John Stevens, *Medieval Romance*, Hutchinson, 1973 (hardback
and paperback).

Sir Gawain and the Green Knight

I

1 Sithen the sege and the assaut was sesed at Troye,
 The burgh brittened and brent to brondes and askes –
 The tulk that the trammes of tresoun there wroght
 Was tried for his trecherye, the truest on erthe –
 Hit was Ennias the athel and his high kynde
 That sithen depresed provinces and patrounes become
 Welnegh of all the wele in the west iles.
 Fro rich Romulus to Rome riches him swythe,
 With grete bobbaunce that burgh he bigges upon first
10 And nevenes hit his owen name, as hit now hat;
 Ticius to Tuskan and teldes begynnes,
 Langaberde in Lumbardie lyftes up homes,
 And fer over the French flode Felix Brutus
 On mony bonkes ful brode Bretayn he settes
        With wynne,
     Where werre and wrake and wonder
     By sythes has woned therinne,
     And oft both blysse and blunder
     Ful skete has skyfted synne.

20 And when this Bretayn was bigged by this burn rich,
 Bold bredden therinne baret that loveden,
 In mony turned tyme tene that wroghten.
 Mo ferlyes on this folde han fallen here oft
 Then in any other that I wot syn that ilk tyme.
 Bot of all that here bult, of Bretayn kynges,
 Ay was Arthur the hendest, as I have herd telle.
 Forthy an aunter in erde I attle to schewe,
 That a selly in sight sum men hit holden
 And an outtrage aventure of Arthures wonderes.
30 If ye wil lysten this laye bot one littel whyle,
 I schal telle hit astit, as I in toun herd,
        With tonge,
     As hit is stad and stoken
     In stori stif and stronge,
     With lel letteres loken
     In londe so has bene longe.

This kyng lay at Camylot upon Cristmasse
With mony lovely lord, ledes of the best,
Rekenly of the Rounde Table all tho rich brether,
40   With rich revel aryght and rechles mirthes.
There tournayed tulkes by tymes ful mony,
Justed ful jolily these gentyle knightes,
Sithen cayred to the court caroles to make.
For there the fest was ilyche ful fiften dayes,
With all the mete and the mirthe that men couth avyse;
Such glaum and gle glorious to here,
Dere dyn upon day, daunsyng on nightes,
All was hap upon high in halles and chambers
With lordes and ladies, as levest hem thoght.
50   With all the wele of the worlde thay woned there samen,
The most kyd knightes under Crystes selven
And the lovelokkest ladies that ever lif haden,
And he the comlokest kyng that the court holdes.
For all was this fayr folk in her first age
          On sille,
     The hapnest under heven,
     Kyng highest mon of wille;
     Hit were now grete nye to neven
     So hardy a here on hille.

60   While Newe Yere was so yep that hit was newe comen,
That day double on the dece was the douth served.
Fro the kyng was comen with knightes into the halle,
The chauntry of the chapel cheved to an ende,
Loude cry was there cast of clerkes and other,
Nowel nayted onewe, nevened ful oft;
And sithen rich forth runnen to reche hanselle,
Yeyed yeres-yiftes on high, yelde hem by hande,
Debated busyly aboute tho giftes;
Ladies laghed ful loude thogh thay lost haden,
70   And he that wan was not wroth, that may ye wel trowe.
All this mirthe thay maden to the mete tyme.
When thay had waschen worthily thay wenten to sete,
The best burn ay above, as hit best semed,

Quene Guenore ful gay graythed in the myddes,
Dressed on the dere dece, dubbed all aboute,
Smal sendal bisides, a selure hir over,
Of tried tolouse and of tars tapites innowe,
That were enbrawded and beten with the best gemmes
That myght be proved of pris with penyes to bye
80   In day.
    The comlokest to discrye
    There glent with yen gray,
    A semloker that ever he sye
    Soth myght no mon say.

Bot Arthur wolde not ete til all were served,
He was so joly of his joyfnes and sumwhat childgered;
His lif liked him lyght, he lovied the lasse
Auther to longe lye or to longe sitte,
So busied him his yong blode and his brayn wylde.
90 And also an other maner meved him eke
That he thurgh nobelay had nomen: he wolde never ete
Upon such a dere day ere him devised were
Of sum aventurus thing an uncouthe tale,
Of sum mayn mervayl that he myght trowe,
Of alderes, of armes, of other aventures,
Auther sum segge him besoght of sum siker knight
To joyne with him in justyng, in jopardy to lay,
Lede, lif for lif, leve uchone other,
As fortune wolde fulsun hem, the fayrer to have.
100 This was kynges countenaunce where he in court were,
At uch farand fest among his fre meyny
      In halle.
    Therfore of face so fere
    He stightles stif in stalle;
    Ful yep in that Newe Yere
    Much mirthe he mas withalle.

Thus there stondes in stalle the stif kyng himselven,
Talkande before the high table of trifles ful hende.
There good Gawayn was graythed Guenore biside,

110 And Agravayn a la dure mayn on that other side sittes,
Both the kynges sistersones and ful siker knightes;
Bischop Bawdewyn above begynnes the table,
And Ywan, Uryn son, ette with himselven.
These were dight on the dece and derworthly served,
And sithen mony siker segge at the sidbordes.
Then the first cource come with crakkyng of trumpes,
With mony baner ful bryght that therbi henged.
Newe nakryn noyse with the noble pipes,
Wylde werbles and wight, wakened lote,
120 That mony hert ful high hef at her towches.
Dayntyes driven therwith of ful dere metes,
Foysoun of the fresch, and on so fele disches
That pine to finde the place the peple before
For to sette the sylveren that sere sewes holden
      On clothe.
    Uch lede as he loved himselve
    There laght withouten lothe;
    Ay two had disches twelve,
    Good ber and bryght wyne both.

130 Now wil I of her servyce say yow no more,
For uch wye may wel wit no wont that there were.
An other noyse ful newe neghed bilive,
That the lede myght have leve liflode to cach;
For unethe was the noyse not a whyle sesed
And the first cource in the court kyndely served,
There hales in at the halle dor an aghlich mayster,
One the most on the molde on mesure high.
Fro the swyre to the swange so sware and so thik
And his lyndes and his lymmes so long and so grete,
140 Half etayn in erde I hope that he were;
Bot mon most I algate mynne him to bene,
And that the meriest in his muckel that myght ride;
For of bak and of brest all were his body sturn,
Both his wombe and his wast were worthily smal
And all his fetures folwande in forme that he had

Ful clene.
For wonder of his hewe men hade,
Set in his semblaunt sene;
He ferde as freke were fade,
150   And overal enker grene.

And all graythed in grene this gome and his wedes:
A strayt cote ful streght that stek on his sides,
A mery mantyle above, mensked withinne
With pelure pured apert, the pane ful clene
With blithe blaunner ful bryght, and his hode both,
That was laght fro his lokkes and layd on his schulderes,
Heme wel-haled hose of that same grene
That spend on his sparlyr, and clene spures under
Of bryght gold upon silk bordes barred ful rich,
160   And scholes under schankes there the schalk rides;
And all his vesture verayly was clene verdure,
Both the barres of his belt and the blithe stones
That were richly rayled in his aray clene
Aboute himself and his sadel upon silk werkes.
That were to tor for to telle of trifles the halve
That were enbrawded above with bryddes and flyes,
With gay gaudi of grene, the gold ay inmyddes.
The pendauntes of his payttrure, the proud cropure,
His molaynes and all the metail anamayld was then,
170   The stiropes that he stode on stayned of the same,
And his arsouns all after and his athel skyrtes,
That ever glemered and glent all of grene stones.
The fole that he ferkes on fyne of that ilk,
Sertayn,
A grene horse grete and thik,
A stede ful stif to strayne,
In brayden brydel quik,
To the gome he was ful gayn.

Wel gay was this gome gered in grene,
180   And the here of his hed of his horse sute.
Fayr fannand fax umbefoldes his schulderes;

A much berd as a busk over his brest henges,
That with his highlich here that of his hed reches
Was evesed all umbetorne above his elbowes,
That half his armes therunder were halched in the wyse
Of a kynges capados that closes his swyre;
The mane of that mayn horse much to hit lyke,
Wel cresped and cemmed, with knottes ful mony,
Folden in with fildore aboute the fayr grene,
190 Ay a herle of the here, an other of gold;
The tayl and his toppyng twynnen of a sute,
And bounden both with a bande of a bryght grene,
Dubbed with ful dere stones, as the dok lasted,
Sithen throwen with a thwong, a thwarle knot aloft,
There mony belles ful bryght of brent gold rungen.
Such a fole upon folde ne freke that him rides
Was never sene in that sale with sight ere that tyme
              With ye.
      He loked as layt so lyght,
200   So sayd all that him sye;
      Hit semed as no mon myght
      Under his dintes drye.

Whether had he no helme ne hauberghe nauther,
Ne no pysan ne no plate that pented to armes,
Ne no schaft ne no schelde to schuve ne to smyte;
Bot in his one hande he had a holyn bobbe,
That is grettest in grene when greves are bare,
And an axe in his other, a huge and unmete,
A spetos sparthe to expoun in spelle, whoso myght.
210 The lenkthe of an elnyerde the large hed had,
The grayn all of grene stele and of gold hewen,
The bit burnyst bryght, with a brode egge
As wel schapen to schere as scharp rasores,
The stele of a stif staf the sturn hit by gripped,
That was wounden with yrn to the wandes ende
And all bigraven with grene in gracious werkes,
A lace lapped aboute that louked at the hed
And so after the halme halched ful oft,

With tried tasseles therto tached innowe
220 On botouns of the bryght grene brayden ful rich.
This hathel heldes him in and the halle entres,
Drivande to the high dece, dutte he no wothe.
Haylsed he never one, bot high he over loked.
The first word that he warp, 'Where is', he sayd,
'The governour of this gyng? Gladly I wolde
Se that segge in syght and with himself speke
    Resoun.'
    To knightes he cast his ye
    And reled hem up and doun;
230   He stemmed and con studie
    Who walt there most renoun.

There was lokyng on lenkthe the lede to behold,
For uch mon had mervayl what hit mene myght
That a hathel and a horse myght such a hewe lach
As growe grene as the gres and grener hit semed,
Then grene aumayl on gold glowande bryghter.
All studied that there stode and stalked him nere
With all the wonder of the worlde what he worch schulde.
For fele sellyes had thay sene, bot such never are;
240 Forthy for fantoum and fayrye the folk there hit demed.
Therfore to answare was arwe mony athel freke
And all stouned at his steven and stone-stille seten
In a swoghe sylence thurgh the sale rich;
As all were slypped upon slepe so slaked her lotes
    In hye.
    I deme hit not all for doute
    Bot sum for cortaysye –
    Bot let him that all schulde loute
    Cast unto that wye.

250 Then Arthur before the high dece that aventure beholdes
And rekenly him reverenced, for rad was he never,
And sayd, 'Wye, welcom iwis to this place.
The hed of this hostel Arthur I hat.

Light lovely adoun and leng, I the pray,
And whatso thy wille is we schal wit after.'
'Nay, as help me,' quoth the hathel, 'he that on high sittes,
To wone any whyle in this wone hit was not myne erande.
Bot for the los of the, lede, is lyft up so high,
And thy burgh and thy burnes best are holden,
260   Stifest under stele-gere on stedes to ride,
The wightest and the worthyest of the worldes kynde,
Preue for to play with in other pure laykes,
And here is kyd cortaysye, as I have herd carp –
And that has wayned me hider iwis at this tyme.
Ye may be siker by this braunch that I bere here
That I passe as in pes and no plyght seche;
For had I founded in fere in fyghtyng wyse,
I have a hauberghe at home and a helme both,
A schelde and a scharp spere schinande bryght,
270   And other weppenes to welde, I wene wel, als;
Bot for I wolde no werre, my wedes are softer.
Bot if thou be so bold as all burnes tellen,
Thou wil graunt me goodly the game that I ask
      By right.'
    Arthur con answare
    And sayd, 'Sir cortays knight,
    If thou crave batayl bare,
    Here fayles thou not to fyght.'

'Nay, frayst I no fyght, in fayth I the telle.
280   Hit are aboute on this bench bot berdles childer.
If I were hasped in armes on a high stede,
Here is no mon me to mach, for myghtes so wayke.
Forthy I crave in this court a Cristmasse game,
For hit is Yol and Newe Yere and here are yep mony.
If any so hardy in this house holdes himselven,
Be so bold in his blode, brayn in his hed,
That dar stifly strike a stroke for an other,
I schal gif him of my gift this giserne rich,
This axe, that is hevy innogh, to hondele as him likes;
290   And I schal bide the first bur as bare as I sitte.
If any freke be so felle to fonde that I telle,

Lepe lyghtly me to and lach this weppen,
I quit-clayme hit for ever, kepe hit as his owen;
And I schal stonde him a stroke stif on this flet,
Elles thou wil dight me the dome to dele him an other,
> Barlay,
>> And yet gif him respite
>> A twelmonyth and a day.
>> Now hye, and let se tite
300 Dar any herinne oght say.'

If he hem stouned upon first, stiller were then
All the heredmen in halle, the high and the lowe.
The renk on his rouncy him ruched in his sadel
And runischly his red yen he reled aboute,
Bende his bresed browes blykkande grene,
Wayved his berd for to wayte whoso wolde rise.
When none wolde kepe him with carp, he coghed ful high
And rimed him ful richly and ryght him to speke:
'What, is this Arthures house', quoth the hathel then,
310 'That all the rous rennes of thurgh ryalmes so mony?
Where is now your surquidry and your conquestes,
Your gryndellayk and your greme and your grete wordes?
Now is the revel and the renoun of the Rounde Table
Overwalt with a word of one wyes speche,
For all dares for drede withoute dint schewed!'
With this he laghes so loude that the lord greved;
The blode schot for schame into his schyre face
> And lere;
>> He wex as wroth as wynde,
320 So did all that there were.
>> The kyng, as kene by kynde,
>> Then stode that stif mon nere,

And sayd, 'Hathel, by heven, thyn askyng is nys,
And as thou foly has frayst, finde the behoves.
I know no gome that is gast of thy grete wordes.
Gif me now thy giserne, upon Goddes halve,
And I schal baythen thy bone that thou boden habbes.'
Lyghtly lepes he him to and laght at his hande.

Then feersly that other freke upon fote lightes.
330 Now has Arthur his axe and the halme grippes
And sturnly stures hit aboute, that strike with hit thoght.
The stif mon him before stode upon hyght,
Herre then any in the house by the hed and more.
With sturn chere there he stode he stroked his berd
And with a countenaunce drye he drow doun his cote,
No more mate ne dismayd for his mayn dintes
Then any burn upon bench had broght him to drynk
        Of wyne.
    Gawayn, that sate by the quene,
340   To the kyng he con enclyne:
    'I beseche now with sawes sene
    This melly mot be myne.

'Wolde ye, worthily lord,' quoth Wawayn to the kyng,
'Bid me bowe fro this bench and stonde by yow there
That I withoute vilany myght voyde this table,
And that my lege lady liked not ille,
I wolde com to your counsel before your court rich.
For me think hit not semly, as hit is soth knowen,
There such an askyng is hevened so high in your sale,
350 Thagh ye yourself be talenttyf, to take hit to yourselven,
While mony so bold yow aboute upon bench sitten,
That under heven I hope none hawerer of wille,
Ne better bodyes on bent there baret is rered.
I am the wakkest, I wot, and of wyt feblest,
And lest lur of my lif, who laytes the soth.
Bot for as much as ye are myne em I am only to prayse,
No bounty bot your blode I in my body knowe.
And sithen this note is so nys that noght hit yow falles,
And I have frayned hit at yow first, foldes hit to me;
360 And if I carp not comlyly let all this court riche
        Bout blame.'
    Rich togeder con roun,
    And sithen thay redden all same
    To ryd the kyng with croun
    And gif Gawayn the game.

Then comaunded the kyng the knight for to rise,
And he ful radly upros and ruched him fayr,
Kneled doun before the kyng and caches that weppen,
And he lovelyly hit him laft and lyft up his hande
370 And gafe him Goddes blessyng and gladly him biddes
That his hert and his hande schulde hardy be both.
'Kepe the, cosyn,' quoth the kyng, 'that thou one kyrf
    sette,
And if thou redes him right, redily I trowe
That thou schal bide the bur that he schal bede after.'
Gawayn gos to the gome with giserne in hande,
And he boldly him bides, he bayst never the helder.
Then carpes to Sir Gawayn the knight in the grene:
'Refourme we oure forwardes ere we fyrre passe.
First I ethe the, hathel, how that thou hattes,
380 That thou me telle truly as I tryst may.'
'In good fayth,' quoth the good knight, 'Gawayn I hat
That bede the this buffet, whatso befalles after,
And at this tyme twelmonyth take at the an other
With what weppen so thou wylt, and with no wye elles
        On live.'
    That other answares ayayn:
    'Sir Gawayn, so mot I thryve
    As I am ferly fayn
    This dint that thou schal drive.

390 'Bigog,' quoth the grene knight, 'Sir Gawayn, me likes
That I schal fonge at thy fust that I have frayst here.
And thou has redily rehersed by resoun ful true
Clanly all the covenaunt that I the kyng asked,
Save that thou schal siker me, segge, by thy trauthe
That thou schal seche me thyself whereso thou hopes
I may be founde upon folde, and foch the such wages
As thou deles me today before this douth rich.'
'Where schulde I wale the?' quoth Gawayn, 'where is thy
    place?
I wot never where thou wones, by him that me wroght,
400 Ne I know not the, knight, thy court ne thy name.

Bot teche me truly therto and telle me how thou hattes,
And I schal ware all my wyt to wynne me thider;
And that I swere the for sothe and by my siker trauthe.'
'That is innogh in Newe Yere, hit nedes no more,'
Quoth the gome in the grene to Gawayn the hende,
'If I the telle truly when I the tappe have
And thou me smothely has smyten, smartly I the teche
Of my house and my home and myne owen name;
Then may thou frayst my fare and forwardes holde.
410 And if I spende no speche, then spedes thou the better,
For thou may leng in thy londe and layt no fyrre.
         Bot slokes!
     Ta now thy grymme tole to the
     And let se how thou knokes.'
     'Gladly, sir, for sothe',
     Quoth Gawayn; his axe he strokes.

The grene knight upon grounde graythly him dresses,
A littel lutte with the hed, the lyre he discoveres,
His long lovely lokkes he layd over his croun,
420 Let the naked nek to the note schewe.
Gawayn gripped to his axe and gederes hit on hyght.
The kay fote on the folde he before sette,
Let hit doun lyghtly light on the naked,
That the scharp of the schalk schyndered the bones
And schrank thurgh the schyre grece and schadde hit in
     twynne,
That the bit of the broun stele bote on the grounde.
The fayr hed fro the halse hitte to the erthe,
That fele hit foyned with her fete there hit forth rolled.
The blode brayde fro the body, that blykked on the grene,
430 And nauther faltered ne fel the freke never the helder,
Bot stythly he start forth upon stif schankes
And runischly he raght out there as renkes stoden,
Laght to his lovely hed and lyft hit up sone,
And sithen bowes to his blonk, the brydel he caches,
Steppes into stele-bawe and strydes aloft,
And his hed by the here in his hande holdes,

And as sadly the segge him in his sadel sette
As none unhap had him ayled, thagh hedles he were
            In stedde.
440   He brayde his bluk aboute,
            That ugly body that bledde;
            Mony one of him had doute
            By that his resouns were redde.

For the hed in his hande he holdes up even,
Toward the derrest on the dece he dresses the face;
And hit lyft up the ye-liddes and loked ful brode
And meled thus much with his mouth as ye may now
            here:
'Loke, Gawayn, thou be grayth to go as thou hettes,
And layt as lelly til thou me, lede, finde,
450   As thou has hette in this halle, herande these knightes.
To the Grene Chapel thou chose, I charge the, to fotte
Such a dint as thou has dalt – disserved thou habbes –
To be yederly yolden on Newe Yeres morn.
The Knight of the Grene Chapel men knowen me mony;
Forthy me for to finde if thou fraystes, fayles thou never.
Therfore com, auther recreaunt be called the behoves.'
With a runisch rout the raynes he turnes,
Haled out at the halle dor, his hed in his hande,
That the fire of the flynt flagh fro fole hoves.
460   To what kyth he become knew none there,
Never more then thay wyste from whethen he was wonnen.
            What then?
            The kyng and Gawayn thare
            At that grene thay laghe and grenne,
            Yet breved was hit ful bare
            A mervayl among tho men.

Thagh Arthur the hende kyng at hert had wonder,
He let no semblaunt be sene, bot sayd ful high
To the comly quene with cortays speche:
470   'Dere dame, today dismay yow never.
Wel becomes such craft upon Cristmasse,
Laykyng of enterludes, to laghe and to syng,

Among these kynde caroles of knightes and ladies.
Never the lasse to my mete I may me wel dresse,
For I have sene a selly, I may not forsake.'
He glent upon Sir Gawayn and gaynly he sayd:
'Now, sir, heng up thyn axe, that has innogh hewen';
And hit was done above the dece on doser to heng,
That all men for mervayl myght on hit loke
480 And by true tytle therof to telle the wonder.
Then thay bowed to a borde these burnes togeder,
The kyng and the good knight, and kene men hem served
Of all dayntyes double, as derrest myght falle.
With all maner of mete and mynstralsye both,
With wele walt thay that day til worthed an ende
        In londe.
    Now thenk wel, Sir Gawayn,
    For wothe that thou ne wonde
    This aventure for to frayn
490   That thou has tan on honde.

II

This hanselle has Arthur of aventures on first
In yong yere for he yerned yelpyng to here.
Thagh him wordes were wane when thay to sete wenten,
Now are thay stoken of sturn werk, stafful her hande.
Gawayn was glad to begynne those games in halle,
Bot thagh the ende be hevy have ye no wonder;
For thagh men bene mery in mynde when thay han mayn
        drynk,
A yere yirnes ful yerne and yeldes never lyke;
The forme to the fynisment foldes ful selden.
500 Forthy this Yol overyede and the yere after,
And uch sesoun serlepes sued after other.
After Cristmasse come the crabbed Lentoun
That fraystes flesch with the fische and fode more symple.
Bot then the weder of the worlde with wynter hit threpes,
Colde clenges adoun, cloudes uplyften,
Schyre schedes the rayn in schowres ful warme,
Falles upon fayr flat, flowres there schewen,

Both groundes and the greves grene are her wedes,
Bryddes busken to bylde and bremely syngen
510   For solace of the soft somer that sues therafter
          By bonk,
      And blossumes bolne to blowe
      By rawes rich and ronk;
      Then notes noble innowe
      Are herd in wode so wlonk.

After the sesoun of somer with the soft wyndes
When Zeferus syfles himself on sedes and erbes,
Wela wynne is the wort that waxes theroute,
When the donkande dewe dropes of the leves,
520   To bide a blysful blusch of the bryght sunne.
Bot then hyes hervest and hardenes him sone,
Warnes him for the wynter to wax ful rype.
He drives with droght the dust for to rise,
Fro the face of the folde to flye ful high;
Wroth wynde of the welkyn wrasteles with the sunne,
The leves lausen fro the lynde and lighten on the grounde,
And all grayes the gres that grene was ere;
Then all rypes and rotes that ros upon first.
And thus yirnes the yere in yisterdayes mony,
530   And wynter wyndes ayayn, as the worlde askes,
          No fage,
      Til Meghelmas mone
      Was comen with wynter wage.
      Then thenkes Gawayn ful sone
      Of his anious vyage.

Yet while All Hal Day with Arthur he lenges;
And he made a fare on that fest for the frekes sake,
With much revel and rich of the Rounde Table.
Knightes ful cortays and comly ladies
540   All for luf of that lede in longynge thay were,
Bot never the lasse ne the later thay nevened bot mirthe;
Mony joyles for that gentyle japes there maden.
For after mete with mournyng he meles to his em

And spekes of his passage, and pertly he sayd:
'Now, lege lord of my lif, leve I yow ask.
Ye know the cost of this case, kepe I no more
To telle yow tenes therof, never bot trifel;
Bot I am boun to the bur barely tomorn,
To seche the gome of the grene, as God wil me wysse.'

550   Then the best of the burgh bowed togeder,
Ywan and Errik and other ful mony,
Sir Doddinaual de Savage, the Duk of Clarence,
Launcelot and Lyonel and Lucan the good,
Sir Boos and Sir Bydver, big men both,
And mony other menskful, with Mador de la Port.
All this compayny of court come the kyng nere
For to counsel the knight with care at her hert.
There was much derne doel driven in the sale
That so worthy as Wawayn schulde wende on that erande

560   To drye a doelful dint and dele no more
        With bronde.
   The knight made ay good chere
   And sayd, 'What schulde I wonde?
   Of destinyes derf and dere
   What may mon do bot fonde?'

He dowelles there all that day and dresses on the morn,
Askes erly his armes, and all were thay broght.
First a tuly tapit tyght over the flet,
And much was the gilt gere that glent theralofte.

570   The stif mon steppes theron and the stele hondeles,
Dubbed in a dublet of a dere tars
And sithen a crafty capados, closed aloft,
That with a bryght blaunner was bounden withinne.
Then set thay the sabatouns upon the segge fotes,
His legges lapped in stele with lovely greves,
With polaynes piched therto polysed ful clene,
Aboute his knes knaged with knottes of gold;
Queme quyssewes then that quayntly closed,
His thik throwen thyghes with thwonges to tached;

580   And sithen the brayden bruny of bryght stele rynges

Umbeweved that wye upon wlonk stuffe,
And wel burnyst brace upon his both armes,
With good cowters and gay and gloves of plate,
And all the goodly gere that him gayn schulde
      That tyde;
  With rich cote-armure,
  His gold spures spend with pryde,
  Gurde with a bronde ful sure
  With silk saynt umbe his side.

590 When he was hasped in armes his harnays was rich;
The lest lachet auther loupe lemed of gold.
So harnayst as he was he herknes his masse
Offred and honoured at the high auter.
Sithen he comes to the kyng and to his court-feres,
Laches lovely his leve at lordes and ladies;
And thay him kyssed and conveyed, bikende him to Cryst.
By that was Gryngolet grayth and gurde with a sadel
That glemed ful gayly with mony gold frenges,
Aywhere nayled ful newe, for that note riched.
600 The brydel barred aboute, with bryght gold bounden;
The apparayl of the payttrure and of the proud skyrtes,
The cropure and the covertour, acorded with the arsouns;
And all was rayled on red rich gold nayles
That all glytered and glent as glem of the sunne.
Then hentes he the helme and hastily hit kysses,
That was stapled stifly and stoffed withinne.
Hit was high on his hed, hasped bihinde
With a lyghtly urysoun over the aventayle,
Enbrawden and bounden with the best gemmes
610 On brode sylkyn borde, and bryddes on semes,
As papjayes paynted pervyng bitwene,
Tortors and truelufes entayled so thik
As mony burde theraboute had bene seven wynter
      In toun.
  The cercle was more of pris
  That umbeclypped his croun,
  Of diamauntes a devys,
  That both were bryght and broun.

Then thay schewed him the schelde, that was of schyre
goules
620　With the pentangel depaynt of pure gold hewes;
He braydes hit by the bauderyk, aboute the halse castes.
That bisemed the segge semlyly fayr;
And why the pentangel apendes to that prynce noble
I am in tent yow to telle, thogh tary hit me schulde.
Hit is a syngne that Salamon set sumwhyle
In bytoknyng of trauthe by tytle that hit habbes;
For hit is a figure that holdes fyve poyntes,
And uch lyne umbelappes and loukes in other,
And aywhere hit is endeles, and Englych hit callen
630　Overal, as I here, the endeles knot.
Forthy hit acordes to this knight and to his clere armes;
For ay faythful in fyve and sere fyve sythes
Gawayn was for good knowen, and as gold pured,
Voyded of uch vilany, with vertues ennourned
　　　　In mote.
　　Forthy the pentangel newe
　　He bere in schelde and cote,
　　As tulk of tale most true
　　And gentylest knight of lote.

640　First he was founden fautles in his fyve wyttes;
And eft fayled never the freke in his fyve fyngeres;
And all his afyaunce upon folde was in the fyve woundes
That Cryst caght on the cros, as the crede telles;
And wheresoever this mon in melly was stad,
His thro thoght was in that, thurgh all other thinges,
That all his forsnes he fong at the fyve joyes
That the hende heven-quene had of hir childe –
At this cause the knight comly had
In the inore half of his schelde hir image depaynted,
650　That when he blusched therto his belde never payred.
The fyft fyve that I finde that the freke used
Was fraunchyse and felawschip forbe all thing,
His clannes and his cortaysye croked were never,
And pity, that passes all poyntes: these pure fyve

Were harder happed on that hathel then on any other.
Now all these fyve sythes for sothe were fetled on this
    knight,
And uchone halched in other that none ende had,
And fyched upon fyve poyntes that fayled never,
Ne samned never in no side, ne sundred nauther,
660 Withouten ende at any noke I oquere finde,
Wherever the game began or glod to an ende.
Therfore on his schene schelde schapen was the knot
Ryally with red gold upon red goules,
That is the pure pentangel with the peple called
       With lore.
   Now graythed is Gawayn gay
   And laght his launce right thore
   And gafe hem all good day,
   He wende for evermore.

670 He sperred the stede with the spures and sprang on his
    way,
So stif that the stone-fire stroke out therafter.
All that sey that semly syked in hert,
And sayd sothly all same segges til other,
Carande for that comly: 'By Cryst, hit is scathe
That thou, lede, schal be lost, that art of lif noble.
To finde his fere upon folde in fayth is not ethe.
Wareloker to have wroght had more wyt bene
And have dight yonder dere a duk to have worthed.
A lowande leder of ledes in londe him wel semes,
680 And so had better have bene then brittened to noght,
Haded with an alvisch mon for angardes pryde.
Who knew ever any kyng such counsel to take
As knightes in cavelaciouns on Cristmasse games!'
Wel much was the warme water that waltered of yen
When that semly syre soght fro tho wones
       That day.
   He made none abode
   Bot wightly went his way.
   Mony wylsum way he rode,
690   The boke as I herd say.

Now rides this renk thurgh the ryalme of Logres,
Sir Gawayn, on Godes halve, thagh him no game thoght.
Oft ledeles alone he lenges on nightes
There he fonde noght him before the fare that he liked.
Had he no fere bot his fole by frythes and downes,
Ne no gome bot God by gate with to carp,
Til that he neghed ful negh into the North Wales.
All the iles of Anglesay on lyft half he holdes
And fares over the fordes by the forlondes,
700   Over at the Holy Hede, til he had eft bonk
In the wyldrenesse of Wyrale: woned there bot lyte
That auther God auther gome with good hert lovied.
And ay he frayned as he ferde at frekes that he met
If thay had herd any carp of a knight grene,
In any grounde theraboute of the Grene Chapel;
And all nikked him with nay, that never in her live
Thay seye never no segge that was of such hewes
            Of grene.
      The knight toke gates straunge
710   In mony a bonk unbene;
      His chere ful oft con chaunge
      That chapel ere he myght sene.

Mony clyff he overclambe in contrayes straunge,
Fer floten fro his frendes fremedly he rides.
At uch warthe auther water there the wye passed
He fonde a foo him before, bot ferly hit were,
And that so foule and so felle that fyght him behoved.
So mony mervayl by mount there the mon findes
Hit were to tor for to telle of the tenthe dole.
720   Sumwhyle with wormes he werres and with wolves als,
Sumwhyle with wodwos that woned in the knarres,
Both with bulles and beres, and bores otherwhyle,
And etaynes that him anelede of the high felle.
Nad he bene doghty and drye and Dryghtyn had served,
Douteles he had bene ded and dreped ful oft;
For werre wrathed him not so much that wynter nas wors,
When the colde clere water fro the cloudes schadde

And fres ere hit falle myght to the fale erthe.
Nere slayn with the slete he slepte in his yrnes
730   Mo nightes then innogh in naked rokkes,
There as claterande fro the crest the colde borne rennes
And henged high over his hede in hard iisse-ikkles.
Thus in peryl and payne and plytes ful hard
By contray cayres this knight til Cristmasse even
      All one.
   The knight wel that tyde
   To Mary made his mone
   That ho him rede to ride
   And wysse him to sum wone.

740   By a mount on the morn meryly he rides
Into a forest ful depe that ferly was wylde,
High hilles on uch a half and holtwodes under,
Of hore okes ful huge a hundreth togeder.
The hasel and the hawthorne were harled all samen,
With rogh raged mosse rayled aywhere,
With mony bryddes unblythe upon bare twyges,
That pitosly there piped for pine of the colde.
The gome upon Gryngolet glydes hem under
Thurgh mony misy and myre, mon all him one,
750   Carande for his costes lest he ne kever schulde
To se the servyce of that syre that on that self night
Of a burde was born oure baret to quelle.
And therfore sykyng he sayd, 'I beseche the, Lord,
And Mary, that is myldest moder so dere,
Of sum herber there highly I myght here masse
And thy matynes tomorn, mekely I ask,
And therto prestly I pray my pater and ave
      And crede.'
   He rode in his prayere
760   And cryed for his mysdede;
   He sayned him in sythes sere
   And sayd, 'Cros Cryst me spede!'

Nad he sayned himself, segge, bot thrye
Ere he was ware in the wode of a won in a mote,
Above a launde on a lawe, loken under boghes
Of mony borelych bole aboute by the diches,
A castel the comlokest that ever knight aghte,
Piched on a prayere, a park all aboute
With a pyked palays pyned ful thik
770 That umbeteye mony tre mo then two myle.
That holde on that one side the hathel avysed,
As hit schemered and schon thurgh the schyre okes;
Then has he hendly of his helme, and highly he thonkes
Jesus and saynt Gilyan that gentyle are both,
That cortaysly had him kyd and his cry herkened.
'Now bone hostel,' quoth the burn, 'I beseche yow yette!'
Then gyrdes he to Gryngolet with the gilt heles,
And he ful chauncely has chosen to the chef gate
That broght bremely the burn to the brygge ende
780   In haste.
    The brygge was breme upbrayde,
    The yates were stoken fast,
    The walles were wel arayed;
    Hit dutte no wyndes blaste.

The burn bode on bonk, that on blonk hoved,
Of the depe double dich that drof to the place.
The walle wod in the water wonderly depe
And eft a ful huge hyght hit haled upon loft,
Of hard hewen stone up to the tables,
790 Enbaned under the abataylment in the best lawe,
And sithen garytes ful gay gered bitwene,
With mony lovely loupe that louked ful clene:
A better barbican that burn blusched upon never.
And innermore he behelde that halle ful high,
Towres telded bitwene, troched ful thik,
Fayr fylyoles that fyed and ferlyly long,
With corven coprounes craftyly sleye.
Chalkwhyte chymnees there ches he innowe,
Upon bastel roves that blenked ful whyte.

800 So mony pynacle paynted was poudred aywhere,
Among the castel carneles clambred so thik,
That pared out of papure purely hit semed.
The fre freke on the fole hit fayr innogh thoght
If he myght kever to com the cloyster withinne,
To herber in that hostel while haliday lasted.
      Avinant.
   He called and sone there come
   A porter pure plesaunt;
   On the walle his erande he nome
810   And haylsed the knight erraunt.

'Good sir,' quoth Gawayn, 'woldes thou go myne erande
To the high lord of this house, herber to crave?'
'Ye, Peter,' quoth the porter, 'and purely I trowe
That ye be, wye, welcom to wone while yow likes.'
Then yede the wye yerne and come ayayn swythe,
And folk frely him with to fonge the knight.
Thay let doun the grete draght and derely out yeden
And kneled doun on her knes upon the colde erthe
To welcom this ilk wye as worthy hem thoght.
820 Thay yolden him the brode yate yarked up wyde,
And he hem raysed rekenly and rode over the brygge.
Sere segges him sesed by sadel while he light,
And sithen stabeled his stede stif men innowe.
Knightes and swyeres comen doun then
For to bryng this burn with blysse into halle.
When he hef up his helme there hyed innowe
For to hent hit at his hande, the hende to serven;
His bronde and his blasoun both thay token.
Then haylsed he ful hendly tho hatheles uchone,
830 And mony proud mon there presed that prynce to honour.
All hasped in his high wede to halle thay him wonnen,
There fayr fire upon flet feersly brenned.
Then the lord of the lede loutes fro his chamber
For to mete with mensk the mon on the flore.
He sayd, 'Ye are welcom to wone as yow likes;
That here is, all is your owen, to have at your wille

                    And welde.'
            'Grant merci,' quoth Gawayn,
            'There Cryst hit yow foryelde.'
840   As frekes that semed fayn
            Ayther other in armes con felde.

        Gawayn glyght on the gome that goodly him gret,
        And thoght hit a bold burn that the burgh aghte,
        A huge hathel for the nones and of high elde.
        Brode, bryght was his berd and all bever-hewed,
        Sturn, stif on the strythe on stalworth schankes,
        Felle face as the fire and fre of his speche;
        And wel him semed for sothe, as the segge thoght,
        To lede a lordschyp in lee of ledes ful good.
850   The lord him charred to a chamber and chefly comaundes
        To delyver him a lede him lowly to serve;
        And there were boun at his bode burnes innowe
        That broght him to a bryght boure there beddyng was
            noble,
        Of cortaynes of clene silk with clere gold hemmes,
        And covertoures ful curious with comly panes
        Of bryght blaunner above, enbrawded bisides,
        Rudeles rennande on ropes, red gold rynges,
        Tapites tyght to the wowe of tuly and tars,
        And under fete on the flet of folwande sute.
860   There he was dispoyled with speches of mirthe,
        The burn of his bruny and of his bryght wedes.
        Rich robes ful rad renkes him broghten
        For to charge and to chaunge and chose of the best.
        Sone as he one hent and happed therinne,
        That sate on him semely with saylande skyrtes,
        The ver by his visage verayly hit semed
        Welnegh to uch hathel, all on hewes,
        Lowande and lovely all his lymmes under,
        That a comloker knight never Cryst made

870   Hem thoght.
            Whethen in worlde he were,
            Hit semed as he moght
            Be prynce withouten pere
            In felde there felle men foght.

       A cheyer before the chymny, there charcole brenned,
       Was graythed for Sir Gawayn graythly with clothes,
       Whyssynes upon queldepoyntes that quaynt were both;
       And then a mery mantyle was on that mon cast
       Of a broun bleaunt, enbrawded ful rich
880   And fayr furred withinne with felles of the best,
       All of ermyn in erde, his hode of the same.
       And he sate in that settel semely rich
       And achaufed him chefly, and then his chere mended.
       Sone was telded up a table on trestes ful fayr,
       Clad with a clene clothe that clere whyte schewed,
       Sanap and salure and sylveren spones.
       The wye wesche at his wille and went to his mete.
       Segges him served semely innowe
       With sere sewes and sete, sesounde of the best,
890   Doublefelde, as hit falles, and fele kyn fisches,
       Sum baken in bred, sum brad on the gledes,
       Sum sothen, sum in sewe savered with spyces,
       And ay sawses so sleye that the segge liked.
       The freke called hit a fest ful frely and oft
       Ful hendly, when all the hatheles rehayted him at ones
               As hende:
            'This penaunce now ye take
            And eft hit schal amende.'
            That mon much mirthe con make
900   For wyne in his hed that wende.

       Then was spied and spured upon spare wyse
       By prevy poyntes of that prynce put to himselven,
       That he beknew cortaysly of the court that he were
       That athel Arthur the hende holdes him one
       That is the rich ryal kyng of the Rounde Table,

And hit was Wawayn himself that in that wone sittes,
Comen to that Cristmasse as case him then lymped.
When the lord had lerned that he the lede had,
Loude laghed he therat, so lef hit him thoght;
910 And all the men in that mote maden much joy
To apere in his presense prestly that tyme
That all pris and prowes and pured thewes
Apendes to his persoun and praysed is ever –
Before all men upon molde his mensk is the most.
Uch segge ful softly sayd to his fere:
'Now schal we semely se slyghtes of thewes
And the techles termes of talkyng noble.
Wich spede is in speche unspured may we lerne,
Syn we have fonged that fyne fader of nurture.
920 God has geven us his grace goodly for sothe,
That such a gest as Gawayn grauntes us to have
When burnes blithe of his burthe schal sitte
          And syng.
    In menyng of maneres mere
    This burn now schal us bryng.
    I hope that may him here
    Schal lern of luf-talkyng.'

By that the diner was done and the dere up
Hit was negh at the night neghed the tyme.
930 Chaplaynes to the chapeles chosen the gate,
Rungen ful richly, right as thay schulden,
To the hersum evensong of the high tyde.
The lord loutes therto and the lady als;
Into a comly closet quayntly ho entres.
Gawayn glydes ful gay and gos thider sone.
The lord laches him by the lappe and ledes him to sitte
And couthly him knowes and calles him his name
And sayd he was the welcomest wye of the worlde;
And he him thonked throly, and ayther halched other
940 And seten soberly samen the servyce whyle.
Then lyst the lady to loke on the knight;
Then come ho of hir closet with mony clere burdes.

Ho was the fayrest in felle, of flesche and of lere
And of compas and colour and costes, of all other,
And wener then Wenore, as the wye thoght.
Ho ches thurgh the chaunsel to cheryse that hende.
Another lady hir lad by the lyft hande
That was older then ho, an auncian hit semed,
And highly honoured with hatheles aboute.
950   Bot unlyke on to loke tho ladies were,
For if the yong was yep, yolwe was that other.
Rich red on that one rayled aywhere;
Rogh ronkled chekes that other on rolled.
Kerchofes of that one with mony clere perles
Hir brest and hir bryght throte bare displayed,
Schon schyrer then snowe that shedes on hilles;
That other with a gorger was gered over the swyre,
Chymbled over hir blake chyn with chalkwhyte vayles,
Hir frount folden in silk, enfoubled aywhere,
960   Toret and treleted with trifles aboute,
That noght was bare of that burde bot the blake browes,
The twayne yen and the nase, the naked lyppes,
And those were soure to se and sellyly blered.
A mensk lady on molde mon may hir calle,
        For Gode.
    Hir body was schort and thik,
    Hir buttokes balwe and brode;
    More lykkerwys on to lyk
    Was that scho had on lode.

970   When Gawayn glyght on that gay that graciously loked,
With leve laght of the lord he lent hem ayaynes.
The older he haylses heldande ful lowe,
The loveloker he lappes a littel in armes.
He kysses hir comlyly and knightly he meles.
Thay callen him of aquoyntaunce, and he hit quik askes
To be her servaunt sothly if hemself liked.
Thay tan him bitwene hem, with talkyng him leden
To chamber, to chymny, and chefly thay asken
Spyces that unsparely men speded hem to bryng,

980 And the wynnelych wyne therwith uch tyme.
The lord lovely aloft lepes ful oft,
Mynned mirthe to be made upon mony sythes,
Hent highly of his hode and on a spere henged,
And wayned hem to wynne the worschyp therof,
That most mirthe myght meve that Cristmasse whyle,
'And I schal fonde, by my fayth, to fylter with the best
Ere me wont the wede, with help of my frendes.'
Thus with laghande lotes the lord hit tayt makes
For to glade Sir Gawayn with games in halle
990   That night,
   Til that hit was tyme
   The lord comaunded light.
   Sir Gawayn his leve con nyme
   And to his bed him dight.

On the morn, as uch mon mynnes that tyme
That Dryghtyn for oure destiny to deye was born,
Wele waxes in uch a wone in worlde for his sake.
So did hit there on that day thurgh dayntyes mony,
Both at messe and at mele messes ful quaynt,
1000 Derf men upon dece dressed of the best.
The olde auncian wyf highest ho sittes,
The lord lovely hir by lent, as I trowe.
Gawayn and the gay burde togeder thay seten
Even inmyddes, as the messe metely come,
And sithen thurgh all the sale as hem best semed.
By uch grome at his degree graythly was served,
There was mete, there was mirthe, there was much joy,
That for to telle therof hit me tene were,
And to poynte hit yet I pined me paraventure.
1010 Bot yet I wot that Wawayn and the wale burde
Such comfort of her compayny caghten togeder
Thurgh her dere dalyaunce of her derne wordes,
With clene cortays carp closed fro fylthe,
That her play was passande uch prynce game

In vayres.
Trumpes and nakerys,
Much pypyng there repayres.
Uch mon tented his
And thay two tented thaires.

1020 Much dut was there driven that day and that other,
And the thrid as thro thronge in therafter:
The joy of saynt Jones day was gentyle to here,
And was the last of the layk, ledes there thoghten.
There were gestes to go upon the gray morn,
Forthy wonderly thay woke and the wyne dronken,
Daunsed ful dryly with dere caroles.
At the last when hit was late, thay lachen her leve,
Uchone to wende on his way that was wye straunge.
Gawayn gafe him good day, the goodmon him laches,
1030 Ledes him to his owen chamber, the chymny biside,
And there he drawes him on drye and derely him
        thonkes
Of the wynne worschyp that he him wayved had,
As to honour his house on that high tyde
And enbelyse his burgh with his bele chere:
'Iwis, sir, while I leve me worthes the better
That Gawayn has bene my gest at Goddes owen fest.'
'Grant merci, sir,' quoth Gawayn, 'in good fayth hit is
        youres,
All the honour is your owen – the high kyng yow yelde.
And I am, wye, at your wille to worch your hest,
1040 As I am holden therto in high and in lowe
        By right.'
    The lord fast con him payne
    To holde lenger the knight.
    To him answares Gawayn
    By none way that he myght.

Then frayned the freke ful fayr at himselven
What derf dede had him driven at that dere tyme
So kenly fro the kynges court to cayre all his one

Ere the halidayes holly were haled out of toun.
1050 'For sothe, sir,' quoth the segge, 'ye sayn bot the
    trauthe.
A high erande and a hasty me had fro tho wones,
For I am sumned myself to seche to a place
I ne wot in worlde whiderwarde to wende hit to finde.
I nolde bot if I hit negh myght on Newe Yeres morn
For all the londe inwith Logres, so me oure lord help.
Forthy, sir, this enquest I require yow here,
That ye me telle with trauthe if ever ye tale herd
Of the Grene Chapel where hit on grounde stondes,
And of the knight that hit kepes, of colour of grene.
1060 There was stabled by statut a steven us bitwene
To mete that mon at that mere, if I myght last;
And of that ilk Newe Yere bot neked now wontes,
And I wolde loke on that lede, if God me let wolde,
Gladloker, by Goddes son, then any good welde.
Forthy, iwis, by your wille, wende me behoves.
Naf I now to busy bot bare thre dayes,
And me as fayn to falle feye as fayly of myne erande.'
Then laghande quoth the lord, 'Now leng the behoves,
For I schal teche yow to that terme by the tymes ende.
1070 The Grene Chapel upon grounde greve yow no more;
Bot ye schal be in your bed, burn, at thyn ese
While forth dayes and ferk on the first of the yere,
And com to that merk at mydmorn to make what yow
    likes
       In spenne.
Dowelles while Newe Yeres day,
And rise and raykes then.
Mon schal yow sette in way;
Hit is not two myle henne.'

Then was Gawayn ful glad and gomenly he laghed:
1080 'Now I thonk yow thryvandely thurgh all other thing.
Now acheved is my chaunce, I schal at your wille
Dowelle and elles do what ye demen.'
Then sesed him the syre and set him biside,

Let the ladies be fette to like hem the better.
There was seme solace by hemself stille;
The lord let for luf lotes so mery
As wye that wolde of his wyt, ne wyst what he myght.
Then he carped to the knight, criande loude:
'Ye han demed to do the dede that I bid.
1090 Wil ye holde this hes here at this ones?'
'Ye, sir, for sothe,' sayd the segge true,
'While I bide in your burgh be bayn to your hest.'
'For ye have travayled,' quoth the tulk, 'towen fro fer,
And sithen waked me with, ye arn not wel waryst
Nauther of sostnaunce ne of slepe, sothly I knowe.
Ye schal leng in your loft and lye in your ese
Tomorn while the messewhyle, and to mete wende
When ye wil with my wyf, that with yow schal sitte
And comfort yow with compayny til I to court turne.
1100　　　Ye lende,
And I schal erly rise;
On huntyng wil I wende.'
Gawayn grauntes all thise,
Him heldande as the hende.

'Yet fyrre,' quoth the freke, 'a forward we make:
Whatsoever I wynne in the wode hit worthes to youres,
And what chek so ye acheve chaunge me therforne.
Swete, swap we so, sware with trauthe,
Whether lede so lymp lere auther better.'
1110 'By God,' quoth Gawayn the good, 'I graunt thertylle,
And that yow lyst for to layke lef hit me thinkes.'
'Who brynges us this beverage, this bargayn is maked',
So sayd the lord of that lede; thay laghed uchone.
Thay dronken and dalyeden and dalten untyghtel,
These lordes and ladies, while that hem liked;
And sithen with Frenkysch fare and fele fayr lotes
Thay stoden and stemmed and stilly speken,
Kysten ful comlyly and caghten her leve.
With mony lede ful lyght and lemande torches
1120 Uch burn to his bed was broght at the last

Ful soft.
To bed yet ere thay yede,
Recorded covenauntes oft;
The olde lord of that lede
Couth wel holde layk aloft.

III

Ful erly before the day the folk uprysen.
Gestes that go wolde her gromes thay calden,
And thay busken up bilive blonkes to sadel,
Tyffen her takles, trussen her males.
1130 Richen hem the richest, to ride all arayed,
Lepen up lyghtly, lachen her brydeles,
Uch wye on his way there him wel liked.
The lef lord of the londe was not the last
Arayed for the ridyng with renkes ful mony;
Ete a sop hastily, when he had herd masse,
With bugle to bent-felde he buskes bilive.
By than that any daylight lemed upon erthe,
He with his hatheles on high horses weren
Then these cacheres that couth coupled her houndes,
1140 Unclosed the kenel dor and called hem theroute,
Blew bigly in bugles thre bare mote.
Braches bayed therfore and breme noyse maked;
And thay chastysed and charred on chasyng that went,
A hundreth of hunteres, as I have herd telle,
Of the best.
To trysters vewters yode,
Couples huntes of kest;
There ros for blastes good
Grete rurd in that forest.

1150 At the first quethe of the quest quaked the wylde;
Dere drof in the dale, doted for drede,
Hyed to the high, bot hetterly thay were
Restayed with the stablye, that stoutly ascryed.
Thay let the herttes have the gate, with the high hedes,
The breme bukkes also with her brode paumes;

For the fre lord had defende in fermysoun tyme
That there schulde no mon meve to the male dere.
The hindes were holden in with 'hay!' and 'ware!',
The does driven with grete dyn to the depe slades.
1160 There myght mon se, as thay slypped, slentyng of
    arewes,
At uch wende under wande wapped a flone,
That bigly bote on the broun with ful brode hedes.
What, thay brayen and bleden, by bonkes thay deyen;
And ay raches in a res radly hem folwes,
Hunteres with high horne hasted hem after
With such a crakkande cry as clyffes haden brusten.
What wylde so atwaped wyes that schotten
Was all toraced and rent at the resayt,
By thay were tened at the high and taysed to the wattres,
1170 The ledes were so lerned at the lowe trysters,
And the grehoundes so grete that geten hem bilive
And hem tofylched as fast as frekes myght loke
      There right.
    The lord for blysse abloy
    Ful oft con lance and light,
    And drof that day with joy
    Thus to the derk night.

Thus laykes this lord by lynde-wodes eves,
And Gawayn the good mon in gay bed lyes,
1180 Lurkes while the daylyght lemed on the wowes
Under covertour ful clere, cortayned aboute.
And as in slomeryng he slode, sleyly he herd
A littel dyn at his dor and dernly open;
And he heves up his hed out of the clothes,
A corner of the cortayn he caght up a littel,
And waytes warely thiderwarde what hit be myght.
Hit was the lady, loveliest to beholde,
That drow the dor after hir ful dernly and stille
And bowed towarde the bed; and the burn schamed
1190 And layd him doun lystily and let as he slepte;
And ho stepped stilly and stel to his bed,

Cast up the cortayn and creped withinne,
And set hir ful softly on the bed-side
And lenged there selly longe to loke when he wakened.
The lede lay lurked a ful long whyle,
Compast in his concience to what that case myght
Meve auther amount; to mervayl him thoght.
Bot yet he sayd in himself, 'More semly hit were
To aspye with my spelle in space what ho wolde.'
1200 Then he wakened and wroth and to hirwarde turned,
And unlouked his ye-liddes and let as him wondered,
And sayned him, as by his sawe the saver to worthe,
                    With hande.
      With chyn and cheke ful swete,
      Both whyte and red in blande,
      Ful lovely con ho lete
      With lyppes smal laghande.

'Good moroun, Sir Gawayn,' sayd that gay lady,
'Ye are a sleper unsleye, that mon may slyde hider.
1210 Now are ye tan astit, bot true us may schape:
I schal bynde yow in your bed, that be ye trayst.'
All laghande the lady laused tho bourdes.
'Good moroun, gay,' quoth Gawayn the blithe,
'Me schal worthe at your wille, and that me wel likes,
For I yelde me yederly and yeye after grace,
And that is the best, by my dome, for me behoves
                    nede.'
And thus he bourded ayayn with mony a blithe laghter.
'Bot wolde ye, lady lovely, then leve me graunt
And deprece your prysoun and pray him to rise,
1220 I wolde bowe of this bed and busk me better;
I schulde kever the more comfort to carp yow with.'
'Nay, for sothe, beau sir,' sayd that swete,
'Ye schal not rise of your bed, I riche yow better:
I schal happe yow here that other half als,
And sithen carp with my knight that I caght have.
For I wene wel, iwis, Sir Wawayn ye are,
That all the worlde worschypes whereso ye ride;

Your honour, your hendelayk is hendly praysed
With lordes, with ladies, with all that lif bere.
1230 And now ye are here, iwis, and we bot oure one;
My lord and his ledes are on lenkthe faren,
Other burnes in her bed and my burdes als,
The dor drawen and dit with a derf haspe.
And sithen I have in this house him that all likes,
I schal ware my whyle wel while hit lastes,
   With tale.
  Ye are welcom to my cors,
  Your owen won to wale;
  Me behoves of fyne force
1240   Your servaunt be, and schale.'

'In good fayth,' quoth Gawayn, 'gayn hit me thinkes,
Thagh I be not now he that ye of speken;
To reche to such reverence as ye reherse here
I am wye unworthy, I wot wel myselven.
By God, I were glad, and yow good thoght,
At sawe auther at servyce that I sette myght
To the plesaunce of your pris; hit were a pure joy.'
'In good fayth, Sir Gawayn,' quoth the gay lady,
'The pris and the prowes that pleses all other,
1250 If I hit lakked auther set at lyght, hit were littel daynty.
Bot hit are ladies innowe that lever were nowthe
Have the, hende, in her holde, as I the have here,
To daly with derely your daynty wordes,
Kever hem comfort and colen her cares,
Then much of the garysoun auther gold that thay haven.
Bot I lowe that ilk lord that the lyft holdes
I have hit holly in my hande that all desyres,
   Thurgh grace.'
  Scho made him so grete chere
1260   That was so fayr of face.
  The knight with speches skere
  Answared to uch a case.

'Madame,' quoth the mery mon, 'Mary yow yelde,
For I have founden in good fayth your fraunchyse noble
And other ful much of other folk fongen by her dedes;
Bot the daynty that thay delen for my disert nis ever –
Hit is the worschyp of yourself, that noght bot wel
 connes.'
'By Mary,' quoth the menskful, 'me think hit an other.
For were I worth all the won of wymmen alyve
1270 And all the wele of the worlde were in my hande,
And I schulde chepen and chose to cheve me a lord,
For the costes that I have knowen upon the, knight, here
Of bewty and debonerty and blithe semblaunt –
And that I have ere herkened, and holde hit here true –
There schulde no freke upon folde before yow be chosen.'
'Iwis, worthy,' quoth the wye, 'ye have waled wel better;
Bot I am proud of the pris that ye put on me
And, soberly your servaunt, my soverayn I holde yow
And your knight I becom, and Cryst yow foryelde.'
1280 Thus thay meled of muchwhat til mydmorn passed,
And ay the lady let lyke as him loved much.
The freke ferde with defence and feted ful fayr;
Thagh ho were burde bryghtest, the burn in mynde had
The lasse luf in his lode for lur that he soght
  Bout hone,
 The dint that schulde him deve,
 And nedes hit most be done.
 The lady then spek of leve;
 He graunted hir ful sone.

1290 Then ho gafe him good day and with a glent laghed,
And as ho stode ho stouned him with ful stor wordes:
'Now he that spedes uch speche this disport yelde yow;
Bot that ye be Gawayn hit gos not in mynde.'
'Wherfore?' quoth the freke, and freschly he askes,
Ferde lest he had fayled in forme of his castes;
Bot the burde him blessed and by this skylle sayd:
'So good as Gawayn gaynly is holden,
And cortaysye is closed so clene in himselven,

Couth not lyghtly have lenged so long with a lady
1300 Bot he had craved a cosse by his cortaysye,
By sum towch of sum trifel at sum tales ende.'
Then quoth Wawayn, 'Iwis, worthe as yow likes.
I schal kysse at your comaundement as a knight falles;
And fyrre, lest he displese yow, so plede hit no more.'
Ho comes nere with that and caches him in armes,
Loutes lovely adoun and the lede kysses.
Thay comly bikennen to Cryst ayther other.
Ho dos hir forth at the dor withouten dyn more,
And he riches him to rise and rapes him sone,
1310 Clepes to his chamberlayn, choses his wede,
Bowes forth when he was boun blithely to masse;
And then he meved to his mete, that menskly him keped,
And made mery all day til the mone rised,
         With game.
   Was never freke fayrer fong
   Bitwene two so dyngne dame,
   The older and the yong;
   Much solace set thay same.

And ay the lord of the londe is lent on his games,
1320 To hunt in holtes and hethe at hindes barayne.
Such a sowme he there slowe by that the sunne helded,
Of does and of other dere, to deme were wonder.
Then feersly thay flokked in, folk at the last,
And quikly of the quelled dere a querry thay maked.
The best bowed therto with burnes innowe,
Gedered the grattest of grece that there were
And didden hem derely undo as the dede askes.
Serched hem at the asay sum that there were,
Two fyngeres thay founde of the foulest of all.
1330 Sithen thay slit the slot, sesed the erber,
Schaved with a scharp knyf and the schyre knitten.
Sithen rytte thay the foure lymmes and rent of the hyde.
Then brek thay the baly, the boweles out token
Lystily for lausyng the lere of the knot.
Thay gripped to the gargulun and graythly departed

The wesaunt fro the wynde-hole and walt out the guttes.
Then schere thay out the schulderes with her scharp
    knyves,
Haled hem by a littel hole to have hole sides;
Sithen brittened thay the brest and brayden hit in twynne.
1340 And eft at the gargulun begynnes one then,
Ryves hit up radly right to the byght,
Voydes out the avanters, and verayly therafter
All the rymes by the rybbes radly thay lause;
So ryd thay of by resoun by the rygge bones
Evendoun to the haunche, that henged all samen,
And heven hit up all hole and hewen hit of there,
And that thay nyme for the noumbles by name, as I
    trowe,
        By kynde.
    By the byght all of the thyghes
1350   The lappes thay lause bihinde;
    To hewe hit in two thay hyes,
    By the bakbon to unbynde.

Both the hed and the halse thay hewen of then,
And sithen sunder thay the sides swyft fro the chyne,
And the corbeles fee thay cast in a greve.
Then thurled thay ayther thik side thurgh by the rybbe
And henged then ayther by hoghes of the fourches,
Uch freke for his fee, as falles for to have.
Upon a felle of the fayr best fede thay thair houndes
1360 With the lyver and the lyghtes, the lether of the
    paunches,
And bred bathed in blode blent theramonges.
Boldly thay blew prys, bayed thair raches,
Sithen fonge thay her flesche, folden to home,
Strakande ful stoutly mony stif motes.
By that the daylight was done, the douth was all wonnen
Into the comly castel, there the knight bides

> Ful stille,
> With blysse and bryght fire bette.
> The lord is comen thertylle;
1370 When Gawayn with him met
> There was bot wele at wille.

Then comaunded the lord in that sale to samen all the
  meyny,
Both the ladies on lowe to light with her burdes.
Before all the folk on the flet frekes he biddes
Verayly his venysoun to fech him before;
And all goodly in game Gawayn he called,
Teches him to the tayles of ful tayt bestes,
Schewes him the schyre grece schorne upon rybbes.
'How payes yow this play? Have I pris wonnen?
1380 Have I thryvandely thonk thurgh my craft served?'
'Ye, iwis,' quoth that other wye, 'here is wayth fayrest
That I sey this seven yere in sesoun of wynter.'
'And all I gif yow, Gawayn,' quoth the gome then,
'For by acorde of covenaunt ye crave hit as your owen.'
'This is soth,' quoth the segge, 'I say yow that ilk:
That I have worthily wonnen these wones withinne
Iwis with as good wille hit worthes to youres.'
He haspes his fayr halse his armes withinne
And kysses him as comlyly as he couth avyse:
1390 'Tas yow there my chevisaunce, I cheved no more.
I wowche hit saf fynly thagh feler hit were.'
'Hit is good,' quoth the goodmon, 'grant merci therfore.
Hit may be such hit is the better, and ye me breve wolde
Where ye wan this ilk wele by wyt of yourselven.'
'That was not forward,' quoth he, 'frayst me no more;
For ye have tan that yow tydes, trowe ye none other
      Ye mowe.'
> Thay laghed and made hem blithe
> With lotes that were to lowe.
1400 To soper thay yede asswythe
> With dayntyes newe innowe.

And sithen by the chymny in chamber thay seten.
Wyes the wale wyne weghed to hem oft,
And eft in her bourdyng thay baythen in the morn
To fylle the same forwardes that thay before maden:
What chaunce so bitydes, her chevisaunce to chaunge,
What newes so thay nome, at night when thay metten.
Thay acorded of the covenauntes before the court all;
The beverage was broght forth in bourde at that tyme.
1410 Then thay lovely laghten leve at the last;
Uch burn to his bed busked bilive.
By that the kok had crowen and cakled bot thryse,
The lord was lopen of his bed, the ledes uchone,
So that the mete and the masse was metely delyvered,
The douth dressed to the wode, ere any day sprenged,
   To chace.
  High with hunte and hornes
  Thurgh playnes thay passe in space,
  Uncoupled among tho thornes
1420 Raches that ran on race.

Sone thay calle of a quest in a kerre side;
The hunte rehayted the houndes that hit first mynged,
Wylde wordes hem warp with a wrast noyse.
The houndes that hit herd hasted thider swythe
And fellen as fast to the fute, fourty at ones.
Then such a glaver and glam of gedered raches
Ros that the rocheres rungen aboute;
Hunteres hem hardened with horne and with mouth.
Then all in a sembly sweyed togeder
1430 Bitwene a flosche in that fryth and a foo cragge;
In a knot by a clyff at the kerre side,
There as the rogh rocher unrydely was fallen,
Thay ferden to the fyndyng, and frekes hem after.
Thay umbekesten the knarre and the kerre both,
Wyes, while thay wysten wel withinne hem hit were
The best that there breved was with the blodhoundes.
Then thay beten on the buskes and bede him upryse,
And he unsoundyly out soght segges overthwert.

One the sellokest swyn swenged out there,
1440 Long sithen fro the sounder that seyed for olde;
For he was a borelych best, bor althergrattest,
Ful grymme when he gronyed. Then greved mony,
For thre at the first thrast he thryght to the erthe
And sparred forth good speed bout spyt more.
These other halowed 'hyghe!' ful high and 'hay! hay!'
    cried,
Haden hornes to mouth, hetterly rechated.
Mony was the mery mouth of men and of houndes
That buskes after this bor with bost and with noyse
        To quelle.
1450   Ful oft he bides the bay
    And maymes the mute in melle.
    He hurtes of the houndes, and thay
    Ful yomerly yaule and yelle.

Schalkes to schote at him schoven to then,
Haled to him of her arewes, hitten him oft;
Bot the poyntes payred at the pyth that pyght in his
    scheldes
And the barbes of his browe bite none wolde;
Thagh the schaven schaft schyndered in peces,
The hed hypped ayayn wheresoever hit hitte.
1460 Bot when the dintes him dered of her drye strokes,
Then braynwod for bate on burnes he rases,
Hurtes hem ful hetterly there he forth hyes,
And mony arwed therat and on lyte drowen.
Bot the lord on a lyght horse lances him after,
As burn bold upon bent his bugle he blowes;
He rechated and rode thurgh rones ful thik,
Suande this wylde swyn til the sunne schafted.
This day with this ilk dede thay driven on this wyse,
Whyle oure lovely lede lyes in his bed,
1470 Gawayn graythly at home in geres ful rich

    Of hewe.
The lady noght foryate
To com him to salue;
Ful erly ho was him at
His mode for to remue.

Ho comes to the cortayn and at the knight totes.
Sir Wawayn hir welcomed worthy on first,
And ho him yeldes ayayn ful yerne of hir wordes,
Settes hir softly by his side and swythely ho laghes,
1480 And with a lovely loke ho layd him these wordes:
'Sir, if ye be Wawayn, wonder me thinkes,
Wye that is so wel wrast alway to good,
And connes not of compaynye the costes undertake,
And if mon kennes yow hem to know, ye cast hem of
    your mynde.
Thou has foryeten yederly that yisterday I taght the
By althertruest token of talk that I couth.'
'What is that?' quoth the wye, 'Iwis I wot never.
If hit be soth that ye breve, the blame is myne owen.'
'Yet I kende yow of kyssyng,' quoth the clere then,
1490 'Whereso countenaunce is couthe quikly to clayme;
That becomes uch a knight that cortaysye uses.'
'Do way,' quoth that derf mon, 'my dere, that speche,
For that durst I not do, lest I devayed were;
If I were werned, I were wrang, iwis, if I profered.'
'Ma fay,' quoth the mery wyf, 'ye may not be werned!
Ye are stif innogh to constrayne with strenkthe if yow
    likes,
If any were so vilanous that yow devaye wolde.'
'Ye, by God,' quoth Gawayn, 'good is your speche,
Bot threte is unthryvande in thede there I lende,
1500 And uch gift that is geven not with good wille.
I am at your comaundement to kysse when yow likes;
Ye may lach when yow lyst and leve when yow thinkes

                    In space.'
          The lady loutes adoun
          And comlyly kysses his face.
          Much speche thay there expoun
          Of druryes greme and grace.

          'I wolde wit at yow, wye,' that worthy there sayd,
          'And yow wrathed not therwith, what were the skylle
1510 That so yong and so yep as ye at this tyme,
          So cortays, so knightyly, as ye are knowen oute –
          And of all chevalry to chose, the chef thing alosed
          Is the lel layk of luf, the lettrure of armes,
          For to telle of this tevelyng of these true knightes,
          Hit is the tyteled token and tyxt of her werkes
          How ledes for her lel luf her lives han auntered,
          Endured for her drury doelful stoundes,
          And after venged with her valour and voyded her care
          And broght blysse into boure with bountyes her owen –
1520 And ye are knight comlokest kyd of your elde,
          Your word and your worschyp walkes aywhere,
          And I have seten by yourself here sere twyes,
          Yet herd I never of your hed helde no wordes
          That ever longed to luf lasse ne more.
          And ye, that are so cortays and quaynt of your hetes,
          Oghe to a yong thing yerne to schewe
          And teche sum tokenes of trueluf craftes.
          Why, are ye lewed, that all the los weldes?
          Auther elles ye demen me to dille your dalyaunce to
              herken?
1530   For schame!
          I com hider sengel and sitte
          To lerne at yow sum game;
          Dos, teches me of your wyt
          While my lorde is fro hame.'

          'In good fayth,' quoth Gawayn, 'God yow foryelde!
          Grete is the good gle and game to me huge
          That so worthy as ye wolde wynne hider

And pine yow with so pore a mon, as play with your
　　knight
With anyskynnes countenaunce, hit keveres me ese.
1540 Bot to take the torvayle to myself to trueluf expoun
And towche the temes of tyxt and tales of armes
To yow, that (I wot wel) weldes more slyght
Of that art, by the half, or a hundreth of such
As I am auther ever schal in erde there I leve,
Hit were a foly felefolde, my fre, by my trauthe.
I wolde your wylnyng worch at my myght,
As I am highly beholden, and evermore wil
Be servaunt to yourselven, so save me Dryghtyn!'
Thus him frayned that fre and fonded him oft
1550 For to have wonnen him to woghe, whatso scho thoght
　　elles.
Bot he defended him so fayr that no faut semed,
Ne none evel on nauther halve, nauther thay wysten
　　　　Bot blysse.
　　Thay laghed and layked longe;
　　At the last scho con him kysse,
　　Hir leve fayr con scho fonge
　　And went hir way, iwis.

Then ruthes him the renk and rises to the masse,
And sithen her diner was dight and derely served.
1560 The lede with the ladies layked all day,
Bot the lord over the londes lanced ful oft,
Sues his uncely swyn, that swynges by the bonkes
And bote the best of his braches the bakkes in sunder
There he bode in his bay, til bawemen hit breken
And made him mawgref his hed for to meve utter,
So fele flones there flete when the folk gedered.
Bot yet the stiffest to start by stoundes he made,
Til at the last he was so mate he myght no more renne,
Bot in the hast that he myght he to a hole wynnes
1570 Of a rasse by a rokk there rennes the borne.
He gete the bonk at his bak, begynnes to scrape,
The frothe femed at his mouth unfayr by the wykes,

Whettes his whyte tusches. With him then irked
All the burnes so bold that him by stoden,
To nye him onferum, bot negh him none durst
    For wothe.
  He had hurt so mony beforne
  That all thoght then ful lothe
  Be more with his tusches torne,
1580 That breme was and braynwod both,

Til the knight come himself cachande his blonk,
Sey him bide at the bay, his burnes biside.
He lightes lovely adoun, leves his corsour,
Braydes out a bryght bronde and bigly forth strydes,
Foundes fast thurgh the forde there the felle bides.
The wylde was ware of the wye with weppen in hande,
Hef highly the here, so hetterly he fnast
That fele ferde for the freke lest fel him the worre.
The swyn settes him out on the segge even,
1590 That the burn and the bor were both upon hepes
In the wightest of the water. The worre had that other,
For the mon merkkes him wel as thay met first,
Set sadly the scharp in the slot even,
Hitte him up to the hult that the hert schyndered,
And he yarrande him yelde and yede doun the water
    Ful tite.
  A hundreth houndes him hent
  That bremely con him bite;
  Burnes him broght to bent
1600 And dogges to dethe endite.

There was blawyng of prys in mony breme horne,
High halowyng on high with hatheles that myght;
Braches bayed that best, as bidden the maysteres,
Of that chargeaunt chace that were chef huntes.
Then a wye that was wys upon wodcraftes
To unlace this bor lovely begynnes.
First he hewes of his hed and on high settes
And sithen rendes him all rogh by the rygge after,

Braydes out the boweles, brennes hem on glede,
1610 With bred blent therwith his braches rewardes.
Sithen he brittenes out the brawne in bryght brode
    scheldes
And has out the hastlettes, as hightly bisemes;
And yet hem halches all hole the halves togeder
And sithen on a stif stange stoutly hem henges.
Now with this ilk swyn thay swengen to home;
The bores hed was born before the burnes selven
That him forferde in the forde thurgh force of his hande
        So stronge.
    Til he sey Sir Gawayn
1620 In halle him thoght ful long.
    He called and he come gayn
    His fees there for to fonge.

The lord ful loude with lote and laghter mery,
When he sey Sir Gawayn, with solace he spekes.
The good ladies were geten and gedered the meyny;
He schewes hem the scheldes and schapes hem the tale
Of the largesse and the lenkthe, the lithernes als,
Of the werre of the wylde swyn in wode there he fled.
That other knight ful comly comended his dedes
1630 And praysed hit as grete pris that he proved had,
For such a brawne of a best, the bold burn sayd,
Ne such sides of a swyn sey he never are.
Then hondeled thay the huge hed, the hende mon hit
    praysed
And let lodly therat the lord for to here.
'Now, Gawayn,' quoth the goodmon, 'this game is your
    owen
By fyne forward and fast, faythely ye knowe.'
'Hit is soth,' quoth the segge, 'and as siker true
All my get I schal yow gif agayn, by my trauthe.'
He hent the hathel aboute the halse and hendly him
    kysses,
1640 And eftersones of the same he served him there.
'Now are we even,' quoth the hathel, 'in this eventide

Of all the covenauntes that we knit sithen I come hider,
  By lawe.'
The lord sayd, 'By saynt Gile,
Ye are the best that I knawe.
Ye bene rich in a whyle,
Such chaffer and ye drawe.'

Then thay telded tables trestes aloft,
Casten clothes upon; clere light then
1650 Wakened by wowes, waxen torches;
Segges sette and served in sale all aboute.
Much glam and gle glent up therinne
Aboute the fire upon flet, and on fele wyse,
At the soper and after, mony athel songes,
As coundutes of Cristmasse and caroles newe,
With all the manerly mirthe that mon may of telle,
And ever oure lovely knight the lady biside.
Such semblaunt to that segge semely ho made,
With stille stollen countenaunce that stalworth to plese,
1660 That all forwondered was the wye and wroth with
  himselven;
Bot he nolde not for his nurture nurne hir ayaynes,
Bot dalt with hir all in daynty, howsoever the dede turned
  Towrast.
 When thay had played in halle
 As longe as her wille hem last,
 To chamber he con him calle,
 And to the chymny thay passed.

And there thay dronken and dalten and demed eft newe
To nurne on the same note on Newe Yeres even;
1670 Bot the knight craved leve to cayre on the morn,
For hit was negh at the terme that he to schulde.
The lord him letted of that, to leng him restayed,
And sayd, 'As I am true segge, I siker my trauthe
Thou schal cheve to the Grene Chapel thy charres to
  make,
Lende on Newe Yeres light longe before pryme.

Forthy thou lye in thy loft and lach thyn ese,
And I schal hunt in this holt and holde the towches,
Chaunge with the chevisaunce, by that I charre hider.
For I have fraysted the twyes and faythful I finde the:
1680 Now "thrid tyme throwe best" thenk on the morn.
Make we mery while we may and mynne upon joy,
For the lur may mon lach whenso mon likes.'
This was graythly graunted and Gawayn is lenged;
Blithe broght was hem drynk, and thay to bed yeden
                With light.
        Sir Gawayn lyes and slepes
        Ful stille and soft all night;
        The lord that his craftes kepes
        Ful erly he was dight.

1690 After masse a morsel he and his men token.
Mery was the morning, his mounture he askes.
All the hatheles that on horse schulde helden him after
Were boun busked on her blonkes before the halle yates.
Ferly fayr was the folde, for the forst clenged;
In red ruded upon rak rises the sunne
And ful clere costes the cloudes of the welkyn.
Hunteres unhardeled by a holt side,
Rocheres rungen by rys for rurd of her hornes.
Sum fel in the fute there the fox bode,
1700 Trayles oft a traveres by traunt of her wyles.
A kenet cries therof, the hunte on him calles;
His felawes fallen him to, that fnasted ful thik,
Runnen forth in a rabel in his right fare,
And he fyskes hem before; thay founden him sone,
And when thay sey him with syght thay sued him fast,
Wreyande him ful weterly with a wroth noyse;
And he trantes and tournayes thurgh mony tene greve,
Havilounes and herkenes by hegges ful oft.
At the last by a littel dich he lepes over a spenne,
1710 Steles out ful stilly by a strothe rande,
Wende have wylt of the wode with wyles fro the houndes.
Then was he went ere he wyst to a wale tryster

There thre thro at a thrich thrat him at ones,
            All gray.
He blenched ayayn bilive
And stifly start onstray;
With all the wo on live
To the wode he went away.

Then was hit list upon live to lythen the houndes,
1720 When all the mute had him met menged togeder.
Such a sorwe at that syght thay sette on his hed
As all the clamberande clyffes had clattered on hepes.
Here he was halowed when hatheles him metten,
Loude he was yayned with yarrande speche;
There he was threted and oft thef called,
And ay the titleres at his tayl, that tary he ne myght.
Oft he was runnen at when he out rayked,
And oft reled in ayayn, so Reynarde was wyly.
And ye he lad hem by lagmon, the lord and his meyny,
1730 On this maner by the mountes while mydoverunder,
While the hende knight at home holsumly slepes
Withinne the comly cortaynes on the colde morn.
Bot the lady for luf let not to slepe,
Ne the purpose to payre that pyght in hir hert,
Bot ros hir up radly, rayked hir thider
In a mery mantyle mete to the erthe,
That was furred ful fyne with felles wel pured;
No houve good on hir hed, bot the hawer stones
Trased aboute hir tressour by twenty in clusteres;
1740 Hir thryven face and hir throte throwen all naked,
Hir brest bare before and bihinde eke.
Ho comes withinne the chamber dor and closes hit hir
            after,
Wayves up a wyndow and on the wye calles,
And radly thus rehayted him with hir rich wordes,
            With chere:
      'A! mon, how may thou slepe,
      This morning is so clere!'
      He was in droupyng depe,
      Bot then he con hir here.

1750 In drye droupyng of dreme draveled that noble,
     As mon that was in mournyng of mony thro thoghtes,
     How that destiny schulde that day dele him his wyrde
     At the Grene Chapel when he the gome metes,
     And behoves his buffet abide withoute debate more.
     Bot when that comly come he kevered his wyttes,
     Swenges out of the swevenes and swares with hast.
     The lady lovely come laghande swete,
     Fel over his fayr face and fetly him kyssed.
     He welcomes hir worthily with a wale chere;
1760 He sey hir so glorious and gayly atyred,
       So fautles of hir fetures and of so fyne hewes,
     Wight wallande joy warmed his hert.
     With smothe smylyng and smolt thay smeten into mirthe,
     That all was blysse and bonchef that brek hem bitwene
               And wynne.
          Thay laused wordes good,
          Much wele then was therinne;
          Grete peryl bitwene hem stode
          Nif Mary of hir knight mynne.

1770 For that prynces of pris depresed him so thik,
     Nurned him so negh the thred, that nede him behoved
     Auther lach there hir luf auther lodly refuse.
     He cared for his cortaysye, lest crathayn he were,
     And more for his meschef if he schulde make synne
     And be traytor to that tulk that that telde aghte.
     'God schylde,' quoth the schalk, 'that schal not befalle.'
     With luf-laghyng a lyte he layd him biside
     All the speches of specialty that sprang of hir mouth.
     Quoth that burde to the burn, 'Blame ye deserve
1780 If ye love not that lif that ye lye nexte,
     Before all the wyes in the worlde wounded in hert,
     Bot if ye have a lemman, a lever, that yow likes better,
     And folden fayth to that fre, festned so hard
     That yow lausen ne lyst – and that I leve nowthe.
     And that ye telle me that now truly I pray yow,
     For all the lufes upon live layne not the soth

           For gile.'
      The knight sayd, 'By saynt Jon,'
      And smethely con he smyle,
1790   'In fayth I welde right none
      Ne none wil welde the whyle.'

    'That is a word,' quoth that wyght, 'that worst is of all;
    Bot I am swared for sothe, that sore me thinkes.
    Kysse me now, comly, and I schal cach hethen;
    I may bot mourne upon molde, as may that much lovies.'
    Sykande ho sweye doun and semely him kyssed,
    And sithen ho severes him fro and says as ho stondes:
    'Now, dere, at this departyng do me this ese,
    Gif me sumwhat of thy gift, thy glove if hit were,
1800 That I may mynne on the, mon, my mournyng to lassen.'
    'Now iwis,' quoth that wye, 'I wolde I had here
    The levest thing for thy luf that I in londe welde,
    For ye have deserved, for sothe, sellyly oft
    More rewarde by resoun then I reche myght.
    Bot to dele yow for drury that dawed bot neked –
    Hit is not your honour to have at this tyme
    A glove for a garysoun of Gawaynes giftes.
    And I am here on erande in erdes uncouthe
    And have no men with no males with menskful thinges;
1810 That mislikes me, lady, for luf at this tyme.
    Uch tulk mon do as he is tan, tas to none ille
          Ne pine.'
      'Nay, hende of high honours,'
      Quoth that lufsum under lyne,
      'Thagh I nad oght of youres,
      Yet schulde ye have of myne.'

    Ho raght him a rich ryng of red gold werkes,
    With a starande stone stondande aloft
    That bere bluschande bemes as the bryght sunne;
1820 Wit ye wel hit was worth wele ful huge.
    Bot the renk hit renayed and redily he sayd:
    'I wil no giftes, for God, my gay, at this tyme;

I have none yow to nurne ne noght wil I take.'
Ho bede hit him ful busyly, and he hir bode wernes
And swere swyftly his soth that he hit sese nolde,
And ho sory that he forsoke and sayd therafter:
'If ye renay my ryng, to rich for hit semes,
Ye wolde not so highly holden be to me,
I schal gif yow my girdel, that gaynes yow lasse.'
1830 Ho laght a lace lyghtly that leke umbe hir sides,
Knit upon hir kyrtel under the clere mantyle –
Gered hit was with grene silk and with gold schaped,
Noght bot arounde brayden, beten with fyngeres –
And that ho bede to the burn and blythely besoght,
Thagh hit unworthy were, that he hit take wolde.
And he nay that he nolde negh in no wyse
Nauther gold ne garysoun ere God him grace sende
To acheve to the chaunce that he had chosen there.
'And therfore, I pray yow, displese yow noght
1840 And lettes be your busynes, for I baythe hit yow never
            To graunt.
      I am derely to yow beholde
      Bicause of your semblaunt,
      And ever in hot and colde
      To be your true servaunt.'

'Now forsake ye this silk,' sayd the burde then,
'For hit is symple in hitself? And so hit wel semes.
Lo, so hit is littel and lasse hit is worthy.
Bot whoso knew the costes that knit are therinne,
1850 He wolde hit prayse at more pris, paraventure;
For what gome so is gurde with this grene lace,
While he hit had hemely halched aboute,
There is no hathel under heven tohewe him that myght,
For he myght not be slayn for slyght upon erthe.'
Then cast the knight, and hit come to his hert
Hit were a juel for the jopardy that him jugged were
When he acheved to the chapel his chek for to fech;
Myght he have slypped to be unslayn the slyght were
      noble.

Then he thulged with hir threpe and tholed hir to speke,
1860 And ho bere on him the belt and bede hit him swythe,
And he graunted and him gafe with a good wille;
And besoght him for hir sake discover hit never,
Bot to lelly layne fro hir lord. The lede him acordes
That never wye schulde hit wit, iwis, bot thay twayne
        For noght.
    He thonked hir oft ful swythe,
    Ful thro with hert and thoght.
    By that on thrynne sythe
    Ho has kyssed the knight so toght.

1870 Then laches ho hir leve and leves him there,
For more mirthe of that mon myght ho not gete.
When ho was gone, Sir Gawayn geres him sone,
Rises and riches him in aray noble,
Lays up the luf-lace the lady him raght,
Hid hit ful holdely there he hit eft fonde.
Sithen chefly to the chapel choses he the way,
Previly aproched to a prest and prayed him there
That he wolde lyste his lif and lern him better,
How his saule schulde be saved when he schulde seye
    hethen.
1880 There he schrof him schyrly and schewed his misdedes,
Of the more and the mynne, and mercy beseches,
And of absolucioun he on the segge calles;
And he asoyled him surely and sette him so clene
As domesday schulde have bene dight on the morn.
And sithen he mas him as mery among the fre ladies,
With comly caroles and all kynnes joy,
As never he did bot that day, to the derk night
        With blysse.
    Uch mon had daynty thare
1890 Of him, and sayd 'Iwis,
    Thus mery he was never are,
    Syn he come hider, ere this.'

Now let him leng in that lee, there luf him bityde.
Yet is the lord on the launde ledande his games.
He has forfaren this fox that he folwed longe.
As he sprent over a spenne to spie the schrewe,
There as he herd the houndes that hasted hem swythe,
Reynarde come richande thurgh a rogh greve,
And all the rabel in a res right at his heles.

1900 The wye was ware of the wylde and warely abides
And braydes out the bryght bronde and at the best
   castes,
And he schunt for the scharp and schulde have arered.
A rach rapes him to right ere he myght,
And right before the horse fete thay fel on him all
And woried me this wyly with a wroth noyse.
The lord lightes bilive and laches him sone,
Rased him ful radly out of the rach mouthes,
Holdes high over his hed, halowes fast,
And there bayen him mony brath houndes.

1910 Huntes hyed hem thider with hornes ful mony,
Ay rechatande aryght til thay the renk seyen.
By that was comen his compayny noble,
All that ever bere bugle blowed at ones
And all these other halowed that had no hornes;
Hit was the meriest mute that ever mon herd,
The rich rurd that there was raysed for Reynarde saule
      With lote.
   Her houndes thay there rewarde,
   Her hedes thay fawne and frote,
1920   And sithen thay tan Reynarde
   And tyrven of his cote.

And then thay helden to home, for hit was negh night,
Strakande ful stoutly in her stor hornes.
The lord is light at the last at his lef home,
Findes fire upon flet, the freke therbiside,
Sir Gawayn the good, that glad was withalle;
Among the ladies for luf he lad much joy.
He were a bleaunt of blue that bradde to the erthe;

His surkot semed him wel that soft was furred,
1930 And his hode of that ilk henged on his schulder;
Blande all of blaunner were both all aboute.
He metes me this goodmon inmyddes the flore,
And all with game he him gret and goodly he sayd:
'I schal fylle upon first oure forwardes nowthe,
That we spedly han spoken there spared was no drynk.'
Then acoles he the knight and kysses him thryse
As saverly and sadly as he hem sette couth.
'By Cryst,' quoth that other knight, 'ye cach much sele
In chevisaunce of this chaffer, if ye had good chepes.'
1940 'Ye, of the chepe no charge,' quoth chefly that other,
'As is pertly payed the porchas that I aghte.'
'Mary,' quoth that other mon, 'myne is bihinde,
For I have hunted all this day and noght have I geten
Bot this foule fox felle – the fende have the goodes! –
And that is ful pore for to pay for such pris thinges
As ye have thryght me here thro, such thre cosses
        So good.'
    'Innogh,' quoth Sir Gawayn,
    'I thonk yow by the rode';
1950   And how the fox was slayn
    He tolde him as thay stode.

With mirthe ana mynstralsye, with metes at her wille,
Thay maden as mery as any men myghten,
With laghyng of ladies, with lotes of bourdes.
Gawayn and the goodmon so glad were thay both,
Bot if the douth had doted auther dronken bene auther.
Both the mon and the meyny maden mony japes,
Til the sesoun was seyen that thay sever most;
Burnes to her bed behoved at the last.
1960 Then lowly his leve at the lord first
Foches this fre mon, and fayr he him thonkes:
'Of such a selly sojourne as I have had here,
Your honour at this high fest, the high kyng yow yelde.
I yef yow me for one of youres, if yourself likes,
For I mot nedes, as ye wot, meve tomorn,

And ye me take sum tulk to teche, as ye hyght,
The gate to the Grene Chapel, as God wil me suffer
To dele on Newe Yeres day the dome of my wyrdes.'
'In good fayth,' quoth the goodmon, 'with a good wille,
1970 All that ever I yow hyght holde schal I redy.'
There asyngnes he a servaunt to sette him in the way
And coundue him by the downes, that he no drech had,
For to ferk thurgh the fryth and fare at the gaynest
    By greve.
  The lord Gawayn con thonk,
  Such worschyp he wolde him weve.
  Then at tho ladies wlonk
  The knight has tan his leve.

With care and with kyssyng he carpes hem til
1980 And fele thryvande thonkes he thrat hem to have,
And thay yelden him ayayn yeply that ilk.
That bikende him to Cryst with ful colde sykynges.
Sithen fro the meyny he menskly departes;
Uch mon that he met, he made hem a thonk
For his servyce and his solace and his sere pine
That thay with busynes had bene aboute him to serve;
And uch segge as sory to sever with him there
As thay had woned worthily with that wlonk ever.
Then with ledes and light he was lad to his chamber
1990 And blithely broght to his bed to be at his rest.
If he ne slepe soundyly say ne dar I,
For he had much on the morn to mynne, if he wolde,
    In thoght.
  Let him lye there stille,
  He has nere that he soght.
  And ye wil a whyle be stille
  I schal telle yow how thay wroght.

IV

Now neghes the Newe Yere and the night passes,
The day drives to the derk, as Dryghtyn biddes.
2000 Bot wylde wederes of the worlde wakened theroute,

Cloudes casten kenly the colde to the erthe,
With nye innogh of the northe the naked to tene;
The snowe snitered ful snart, that snayped the wylde;
The werbelande wynde wapped fro the high
And drof uch dale ful of dryftes ful grete.
The lede lystened ful wel that lay in his bed,
Thagh he loukes his liddes ful littel he slepes;
By uch kok that crue he knew wel the steven.
Deliverly he dressed up ere the day sprenged,
2010 For there was light of a laumpe that lemed in his chamber.
He called to his chamberlayn, that cofly him swared,
And bede him bryng him his bruny and his blonk sadel.
That other ferkes him up and feches him his wedes
And graythes me Sir Gawayn upon a grete wyse.
First he clad him in his clothes the colde for to were,
And sithen his other harnays, that holdely was keped,
Both his paunce and his plates piked ful clene,
The rynges rokked of the roust of his rich bruny;
And all was fresch as upon first, and he was fayn then
2020   To thonk.
        He had upon uch pece,
        Wypped ful wel and wlonk,
        The gayest into Grece;
        The burn bede bryng his blonk.

While the wlonkest wede he warp on himselven,
His cote with the conysaunce of the clere werkes
Ennourned upon velvet, vertuus stones
Aboute beten and bounden, enbrawded semes,
And fayr furred withinne with fayr pelures,
2030 Yet laft he not the lace, the ladies gift –
That forgat not Gawayn for good of himselven.
By he had belted the bronde upon his balwe haunches,
Then dressed he his drury double him aboute,
Swythe swethled umbe his swange swetely that knight.
The girdel of the grene silk that gay wel bisemed,
Upon that ryal red clothe that rich was to schewe.
Bot wered not this ilk wye for wele this girdel,

For pryde of the pendauntes, thagh polysed thay were,
And thagh the glyterande gold glent upon endes,
2040 Bot for to saven himself when suffer him behoved,
To bide bale withoute debate, of bronde him to were
Auther knyve.
By that the bold mon boun
Wynnes theroute bilive,
All the meyny of renoun
He thonkes oft ful ryve.

Then was Gryngolet grayth, that grete was and huge,
And had bene sojourned saverly and in a siker wyse;
Him lyst prik for poynt, that proud horse then.
2050 The wye wynnes him to and wytes on his lyre,
And sayd soberly himself and by his soth sweres:
'Here is a meyny in this mote that on mensk thenkes.
The mon hem maynteines, joy mot he have!
The lef lady on live, luf hir bityde!
If thay for charyty cherysen a gest
And holden honour in her hande, the hathel hem yelde
That holdes the heven upon high, and also yow all!
And if I myght lif upon londe lede any whyle,
I schulde reche yow sum rewarde redily if I myght.'
2060 Then steppes he into stirop and strydes aloft;
His schalk schewed him his schelde, on schulder he hit
laght,
Gyrdes to Gryngolet with his gilt heles,
And he startes on the stone, stode he no lenger
To praunce.
His hathel on horse was then,
That bere his spere and launce.
'This castel to Cryst I kenne;
He gif hit ay good chaunce.'

The brygge was brayde doun and the brode yates
2070 Unbarred and borne open upon both halve.
The burn blessed him bilive and the bredes passed,
Prayses the porter – before the prynce kneled,

Gafe him God and good day, that Gawayn he save –
And went on his way with his wye one,
That schulde teche him to turne to that tene place
There the ruful race he schulde resayve.
Thay bowen by bonkes there boghes are bare,
Thay clomben by clyffes there clenges the colde.
The heven was uphalt, bot ugly therunder.
2080 Mist muged on the mor, malt on the mountes,
Uch hille had a hatte, a mist-hakel huge.
Brokes boyled and brek by bonkes aboute,
Schyre schaterande on schores there thay doun schuved.
Wela wylle was the way there thay by wode schulden,
Til hit was sone sesoun that the sunne rises
       That tyde.
    Thay were on a hille ful high,
    The whyte snowe lay biside.
    The burn that rode him by
2090   Bede his mayster abide,

'For I have wonnen yow hider, wye, at this tyme,
And now nare ye not fer fro that note place
That ye han spied and spured so specially after.
Bot I schal say yow for sothe, sithen I yow know
And ye are a lede upon live that I wel lovie;
Wolde ye worch by my wyt, ye worthed the better.
The place that ye prese to ful perelous is holden.
There wones a wye in that waste the worst upon erthe,
For he is stif and sturn and to strike lovies,
2100 And more he is then any mon upon myddelerde,
And his body bigger then the best foure
That are in Arthures house, Hestor auther other.
He cheves that chaunce at the Chapel Grene,
There passes none by that place so proud in his armes
That he ne dynges him to dethe with dint of his hande,
For he is a mon methles and mercy none uses.
For be hit chorle auther chaplayn that by the chapel rides,
Monk auther masseprest auther any mon elles,
Him think as queme him to quelle as quik go himselven.

2110 Forthy I say the as soth as ye in sadel sitte,
     Com ye there, ye be kylled, may the knight rede,
     Trowe ye me that truly, thagh ye had twenty lives
         To spende.
     He has woned here ful yore,
     On bent much baret bende;
     Ayayn his dintes sore
     Ye may not yow defende.

     'Forthy, good Sir Gawayn, let the gome one
     And gos away sum other gate, upon Goddes halve.
2120 Cayres by sum other kyth, there Cryst mot yow spede,
     And I schal hye me home ayayn, and hete yow fyrre
     That I schal swere by God and all his good halwes,
     As help me God and the halydam, and othes innowe,
     That I schal lelly yow layne and lause never tale
     That ever ye founded to fle for freke that I wyst.'
     'Grant merci,' quoth Gawayn, and gruchyng he sayd,
     'Wel worthe the, wye, that woldes my good,
     And that lelly me layne I leve wel thou woldes.
     Bot helde thou hit never so holde, and I here passed,
2130 Founded for ferde for to fle in forme that thou telles,
     I were a knight cowarde, I myght not be excused.
     Bot I wil to the chapel, for chaunce that may falle,
     And talk with that ilk tulk the tale that me lyst,
     Worth hit wele auther wo, as the wyrde likes
         Hit have.
     Thagh he be a sturn knape
     To stightel, and stad with stave,
     Ful wel con Dryghtyn schape
     His servauntes for to save.'

2140 'Mary!' quoth that other mon, 'now thou so much
         spelles
     That thou wylt thyn owen nye nyme to thyselven,
     And the lyst lese thy lif, the lette I ne kepe.
     Have here thy helme on thy hed, thy spere in thy hande,
     And ride me doun this ilk rake by yon rokk side

Til thou be broght to the bothem of the breme valay.
Then loke a littel on the launde on thy lyft hande,
And thou schal se in that slade the self chapel
And the borelych burn on bent that hit kepes.
Now fares wel on Goddes halve, Gawayn the noble;
2150 For all the gold upon grounde I nolde go with the,
Ne bere the felawschip thurgh this fryth one fote fyrre.'
By that the wye in the wode wendes his brydel,
Hitte the horse with the heles as hard as he myght,
Lepes him over the launde and leves the knight there
       All one.
    'By Goddes self,' quoth Gawayn,
    'I wil nauther grete ne grone.
    To Goddes wille I am ful bayn,
    And to him I have me tone.'

2160 Then gyrdes he to Gryngolet and gederes the rake,
Schuves in by a schore at a schawe side,
Rides thurgh the rogh bonk right to the dale.
And then he wayted him aboute, and wylde hit him
    thoght,
And sey no syngne of resette bisides nowhere,
Bot high bonkes and brent upon both halve
And rogh knokled knarres with knorned stones;
The skues of the scowtes skayned him thoght.
Then he hoved and withhelde his horse at that tyde,
And oft chaunged his chere the chapel to seche.
2170 He sey none such in no side, and selly him thoght,
Save a littel on a launde, a lawe as it were,
A balwe berwe by a bonk the brymme biside,
By a forw of a flode that ferked thare;
The borne blubred therinne as hit boyled had.
The knight caches his caple and come to the lawe,
Lightes doun lovelyly and at a lynde taches
The rayne, and hit riches with a rogh braunch.
Then he bowes to the berwe, aboute hit he walkes,
Debatande with himself what hit be myght.
2180 Hit had a hole on the ende and on ayther side,

And overgrowen with gres in glodes aywhere,
And all was holw inwith, nobot an olde cave
Or a crevisse of an olde cragge, he couth hit noght deme
   With spelle.
 'We! Lord,' quoth the gentyle knight,
 'Whether this be the Grene Chapel?
 Here myght aboute mydnight
 The Devel his matynes telle.

 'Now iwis,' quoth Wawayn, 'wysty is here.
2190 This oritore is ugly, with erbes overgrowen;
Wel bisemes the wye wruxled in grene
Dele here his devocioun on the Develes wyse.
Now I fele hit is the fende, in my fyve wyttes,
That has stoken me this steven to strye me here.
This is a chapel of meschaunce, that chek hit bityde!
Hit is the corsedest kyrk that ever I come inne.'
With high helme on his hed, his launce in his hande,
He romes up to the roffe of tho rogh wones.
Then herd he of that high hille, in a hard roche,
2200 Biyonde the broke in a bonk, a wonder breme noyse.
What, hit clatered in the clyff as hit cleve schulde,
As one upon a gryndelston had grounden a sythe;
What, hit wharred and whette as water at a mulne;
What, hit rusched and ronge, rawthe to here.
Then 'By God,' quoth Gawayn, 'that gere, as I trowe,
Is riched at the reverence me, renk, to mete
  By rote.
 Let God worch! We loo!
 Hit helpes me not a mote.
2210 My lif thagh I forgoo,
 Drede dos me no lote.'

Then the knight con calle ful high:
'Who stightles in this stedde me steven to holde?
For now is good Gawayn goande right here.
If any wye oght wil, wynne hider fast,
Auther now auther never, his nedes to spede.'

'Abide,' quoth one on the bonk aboven over his hed,
'And thou schal have all in hast that I the hyght ones.'
Yet he rusched on that rurd rapely a throwe
2220 And with whettyng awharf ere he wolde light;
And sithen he keveres by a cragge and comes of a hole,
Whyrlande out of a wro with a felle weppen,
A denes axe newe dight the dint with to yelde,
With a borelych bit bende by the halme,
Fyled in a fylor, foure fote large –
Hit was no lasse, by that lace that lemed ful bryght!
And the gome in the grene gered as first,
Both the lere and the legges, lokkes and berd,
Save that fayr on his fote he foundes on the erthe,
2230 Sette the stele to the stone and stalked biside.
When he wan to the water, there he wade nolde,
He hypped over on his axe and orpedly strydes,
Bremely brath on a bent that brode was aboute
        On snowe.
    Sir Gawayn the knight con mete,
    He ne lutte him nothyng lowe.
    That other sayd, 'Now, sir swete,
    Of steven mon may the trowe.

'Gawayn,' quoth that grene gome, 'God the mot loke!
2240 Iwis thou art welcom, wye, to my place,
And thou has tymed thy travayl as true mon schulde,
And thou knowes the covenauntes cast us bitwene:
At this tyme twelmonyth thou toke that the falled,
And I schulde at this Newe Yere yeply the quyte.
And we are in this valay verayly oure one;
Here are no renkes us to ryd, rele as us likes.
Have thy helme of thy hed and have here thy pay.
Busk no more debate then I the bede then
When thou wypped of my hed at a wap one.'
2250 'Nay, by God,' quoth Gawayn, 'that me gost lante,
I schal gruch the no grue for greme that falles.
Bot stightel the upon one stroke, and I schal stonde stille
And warp the no wernyng to worch as the likes

Nowhare.'
He lened with the nek and lutte
And schewed that schyre all bare
And let as he noght dutte;
For drede he wolde not dare.

Then the gome in the grene graythed him swythe,
2260 Gederes up his grymme tole Gawayn to smyte;
With all the bur in his body he bere hit on loft,
Mynt as maghtyly as marre him he wolde.
Had hit driven adoun as drye as he attled,
There had bene ded of his dint that doghty was ever;
Bot Gawayn on that giserne glyfte him biside,
As hit come glydande adoun on glode him to schende,
And schrank a littel with the schulderes for the scharp
     yrn.
That other schalk with a schunt the schene withholdes,
And then repreved he the prynce with mony proud
     wordes:
2270 'Thou art not Gawayn,' quoth the gome, 'that is so good
     holden,
That never arwed for no here by hille ne by vale,
And now thou fles for ferde ere thou fele harmes!
Such cowardise of that knight couth I never here.
Nauther fyked I ne flagh, freke, when thou myntest,
Ne cast no cavelacioun in kynges house Arthur.
My hed flagh to my fote and yet flagh I never,
And thou, ere any harme hent, arwes in hert;
Wherfore the better burn me burde be called
          Therfore.'
2280 Quoth Gawayn, 'I schunt ones,
     And so wil I no more.
Bot thagh my hed falle on the stones
     I con not hit restore.

'Bot busk, burn, by thy fayth, and bryng me to the poynt,
Dele to me my destiny and do hit out of hande;
For I schal stonde the a stroke and start no more

Til thyn axe have me hitte, have here my trauthe.'
'Have at the then!' quoth that other, and heves hit aloft
And waytes as wrothly as he wode were.
2290 He myntes at him maghtyly bot not the mon rynes,
Withhelde hetterly his hande ere hit hurt myght.
Gawayn graythly hit bides and glent with no membre,
Bot stode stille as the stone, auther a stubbe auther
That ratheled is in rochy grounde with rotes a hundreth.
Then meryly eft con he mele, the mon in the grene:
'So, now thou has thy hert hole, hitte me behoves.
Holde the now the high hode that Arthur the raght,
And kepe thy kanel at this cast, if hit kever may.'
Gawayn ful gryndelly with greme then sayd:
2300 'Wy! thresch on, thou thro mon, thou thretes to longe.
I hope that thy hert arwe with thyn owen selven.'
'For sothe,' quoth that other freke, 'so felly thou spekes,
I wil no lenger on lyte lette thyn erande
            Right now.'
      Then tas he him strythe to strike
      And frounses both lyppe and browe.
      No mervayl thagh him mislike
      That hoped of no rescowe.

He lyftes lyghtly his lome and let hit doun fayr
2310 With the barbe of the bit by the bare nek;
Thagh he homered hetterly, hurt him no more
Bot snyrt him on that one side, that severed the hyde.
The scharp schrank to the flesch thurgh the schyre grece,
That the schene blode over his schulderes schot to the erthe.
And when the burn sey the blode blenk on the snowe,
He sprit forth spenne-fote more then a spere lenkthe,
Hent hetterly his helme and on his hed cast,
Schot with his schulderes his fayr schelde under,
Braydes out a bryght bronde, and bremely he spekes –
2320 Never syn that he was burn born of his moder
Was he never in this worlde wye half so blithe –
'Blynne, burn, of thy bur, bede me no mo!
I have a stroke in this stedde withoute stryf hent,

And if thou reches me any mo, I redily schal quyte
And yelde yederly ayayn, and therto ye tryst –
  And foo.
 Bot one stroke here me falles;
 The covenaunt schop right so
 Festned in Arthures halles;
2330 And therfore, hende, now hoo!'

The hathel helded him fro and on his axe rested,
Sette the schaft upon schore and to the scharp lened
And loked to the lede that on the launde yede,
How that doghty dredles derfly there stondes
Armed, ful awles; in hert hit him likes.
Then he meles meryly with a much steven
And with a ryngande rurd he to the renk sayd:
'Bold burn on this bent be not so gryndel.
No mon here unmanerly the mysboden habbes,
2340 Ne kyd bot as covenaunt at kynges court schaped.
I hyght the a stroke and thou hit has; holde the wel payed.
I relece the of the remnaunt of rightes all other.
If I deliver had bene, a buffet paraventure
I couth wrothloker have wared, to the have wroght anger.
First I mansed the meryly with a mynt one
And rove the with no rof-sore, with right I the profered
For the forward that we fest in the first night,
And thou trystyly the trauthe and truly me holdes;
All the gayne thou me gafe as good mon schulde.
2350 That other mynt for the morn, mon, I the profered;
Thou kyssedes my clere wyf, the cosses me raghtes.
For both two here I the bede bot two bare myntes
  Bout scathe.
 True mon true restore,
 Then thar mon drede no wathe.
 At the thrid thou fayled thore,
 And therfore that tappe ta the.

'For hit is my wede that thou weres, that ilk woven
 girdel,

Myne owen wyf hit the weved, I wot wel for sothe.
2360 Now know I wel thy cosses and thy costes als,
And the wowyng of my wyf, I wroght hit myselven.
I sende hir to assay the, and sothly me thinkes
One the fautlest freke that ever on fote yede.
As perle by the whyte pese is of pris more,
So is Gawayn in good fayth by other gay knightes.
Bot here yow lakked a littel, sir, and lewty yow wonted;
Bot that was for no wylede werk, ne wowyng nauther,
Bot for ye loved your lif – the lasse I yow blame.'
That other stif mon in study stode a grete whyle,
2370 So agreved for greme he gryed withinne;
All the blode of his brest blent in his face,
That all he schrank for schame that the schalk talked.
The forme word upon folde that the freke meled:
'Corsed worth cowardise and covetyse both!
In yow is vilany and vyse that vertue disstryes.'
Then he caght to the knot and the cast lauses,
Brayde brathly the belt to the burn selven:
'Lo, there the falssyng, foule mot hit falle!
For care of thy knokke cowardise me taght
2380 To acorde me with covetyse, my kynde to forsake,
That is largesse and lewty that longes to knightes.
Now am I fauty and falce, and ferde have bene ever
Of trecherye and untrauthe – both bityde sorwe
        And care!
    I beknowe yow, knight, here stille,
    All fauty is my fare.
    Letes me overtake your wille
    And eft I schal be ware.'

Then loghe that other lede and lovelyly sayd:
2390 'I holde hit hardily hole the harme that I had;
Thou art confessed so clene, beknowen of thy mysses,
And has the penaunce apert of the poynt of myne egge.
I holde the polysed of that plyght and pured as clene
As thou hades never forfeted sithen thou was first born.
And I gif the, sir, the girdel that is gold-hemmed;

For hit is grene as my goune, Sir Gawayn, ye may
Thenk upon this ilk threpe there thou forth thrynges
Among prynces of pris, and this a pure token
Of the chaunce of the Grene Chapel at chevalrous
    knightes.
2400 And ye schal in this Newe Yere ayayn to my wones,
And we schal revel the remnaunt of this rich fest
       Ful bene.'
   There lathed him fast the lord
   And sayd, 'With my wyf, I wene,
   We schal yow wel acorde,
   That was your enmy kene.'

'Nay, for sothe,' quoth the segge, and sesed his helme
And has hit of hendly and the hathel thonkes:
'I have sojourned sadly; sele yow bityde
2410 And he yelde hit yow yare that yarkes all menskes!
And comaundes me to that cortays, your comly fere,
Both that one and that other, myne honoured ladies,
That thus her knight with her cast han quayntly bigyled.
Bot hit is no ferly thagh a fole madde,
And thurgh wyles of wymmen bè wonnen to sorwe;
For so was Adam in erde with one bigyled,
And Salamon with fele sere; and Samson eftsones,
Dalyda dalt him his wyrde; and Davyth therafter
Was blended with Barsabe, that much bale tholed.
2420 Now these were wrathed with her wyles, hit were a wynne
    huge
To love hem wel and leve hem not, a lede that couth.
For these were forne the freest, that folwed all the sele
Exellently of all these other under hevenryche
      That mused;
   And all thay were biwyled
   With wymmen that thay used.
   Thagh I be now bigyled,
   Me think me burde be excused.

'Bot your girdel,' quoth Gawayn, 'God yow foryelde!
2430 That wil I welde with good wille, not for the wynne gold,
Ne the saynt, ne the silk, ne the syde pendauntes,
For wele ne for worschyp, ne for the wlonk werkes,
Bot in syngne of my surfet I schal se hit oft,
When I ride in renoun remorde to myselven
The faut and the fayntyse of the flesche crabbed,
How tender hit is to entyse teches of fylthe;
And thus, when pryde schal me prik for prowes of armes,
The loke to this luf-lace schal lethe my hert.
Bot one I wolde yow pray, displeses yow never:
2440 Syn ye be lord of the yonder londe that I have lent inne
With yow with worschyp – the wye hit yow yelde
That upholdes the heven and on high sittes –
How nurne ye your right name, and then no more?'
'That schal I telle the truly,' quoth that other then:
'Bertilak de Hautdesert I hat in this londe.
Thurgh myght of Morgne la Faye, that in my house
     lenges,
And koyntyse of clergye by craftes wel lerned,
The maystryes of Merlyn mony has taken;
For ho has dalt drury ful dere sumtyme
2450 With that conable clerk, that knowes all your knightes
          At hame.
     Morgne the goddes
     Therfore hit is hir name;
     Weldes none so high hawtesse
     That ho ne con make ful tame.

'Ho wayned me upon this wise to your wynne halle
For to assay the surquidry, if hit soth were
That rennes of the grete renoun of the Rounde Table.
Ho wayned me this wonder your wyttes to reve,
2460 For to have greved Guenore and gard hir to deye
With glopnyng of that ilk gome that gostlych speked
With his hed in his hande before the high table.
That is ho that is at home, the auncian lady;
Ho is even thyn aunt, Arthures half-suster,

The Duches doghter of Tyntagelle, that dere Uter after
Had Arthur upon, that athel is nowthe.
Therfore I ethe the, hathel, to com to thyn aunt,
Make mery in my house; my meyny the lovies,
And I wil the as wel, wye, by my fayth,
2470 As any gome under God, for thy grete trauthe.'
And he nikked him nay, he nolde by no wayes.
Thay acolen and kyssen, bikennen ayther other
To the prynce of paradise, and parten right there
On colde.
    Gawayn on blonk ful bene
    To the kynges burgh buskes bolde,
    And the knight in the enker grene
    Whiderwarde-so-ever he wolde.

Wylde wayes in the worlde Wawayn now rides
2480 On Gryngolet, that the grace had geten of his live.
Oft he herbered in house and oft all theroute,
And mony aventure in vale he venquyst oft
That I ne tyght at this tyme in tale to remene.
The hurt was hole that he had hent in his nek,
And the blykkande belt he bere theraboute
Abelef as a bauderyk bounden by his side,
Loken under his lyft arme, the lace, with a knot,
In tokenyng he was tan in tech of a faut;
And thus he comes to the court, knight all in sounde.
2490 There wakened wele in that wone when wyst the grete
That good Gawayn was comen; gayn hit hem thoght.
The kyng kysses the knight, and the quene als,
And sithen mony siker knight that soght him to haylse,
Of his fare that him frayned; and ferlyly he telles,
Beknowes all the costes of care that he had,
The chaunce of the chapel, the chere of the knight,
The luf of the lady, the lace at the last.
The nirt in the nek he naked hem schewed
That he laght for his unlewty at the ledes handes

2500   For blame.
    He tened when he schulde telle,
    He groned for gref and grame;
    The blode in his face con melle
    When he hit schulde schewe for schame.

    'Lo, lord,' quoth the lede, and the lace hondeled,
    'This is the bende of this blame I bere in my nek;
    This is the lothe and the losse that I laght have
    Of cowardise and covetyse that I have caght thare;
    This is the token of untrauthe that I am tan inne,
2510 And I mot nedes hit were while I may last.
    For none may hyden his harme bot unhap ne may hitte,
    For there hit ones is tached twynne wil hit never.'
    The kyng comfortes the knight, and all the court als,
    Laghen loude therat and lovelyly acorden
    That lordes and ledes that longed to the Table,
    Uch burn of the brotherhede, a bauderyk schulde have,
    A bende abelef him aboute of a bryght grene,
    And that for sake of that segge in sute to were.
    For that was acorded the renoun of the Rounde Table
2520 And he honoured that hit had evermore after,
    As hit is breved in the best boke of romaunce.
    Thus in Arthures day this aunter bitidde,
    The Brutus bokes therof beres wyttenesse.
    Sithen Brutus the bold burn bowed hider first,
    After the sege and the assaut was sesed at Troye,
        Iwis,
    Mony aunteres here beforne
    Have fallen such ere this.
    Now that bere the croun of thorne,
2530 He bryng us to his blysse.   AMEN

HONY SOYT QUI MAL PENCE

Notes

1–7 The main sentence runs as follows: 'After the siege and the assault had finished at Troy and the city had been broken up and burnt to charred wood and ashes . . . it was the noble Aeneas and his lofty kindred who afterwards conquered provinces and became lords of nearly all the wealth of the lands of the west.' Virgil's story of the foundation of the Roman Empire by Aeneas inspired later writers to derive other European realms from the same stock: hence the 'lofty kindred', some of whom are named in the lines which follow.

3–4 This parenthesis would probably have been understood as a reference to Antenor, who was the Trojan most concerned in betraying Troy to the Greeks and so became 'famous for his treachery, the veriest example on earth'. Aeneas himself, however, was also involved in the betrayal, according to some accounts. The point of the parenthesis is to introduce the idea of treachery, a vice which, being opposed to the virtue of 'trauthe' (see 2383), represents one of the poem's important themes.

8 *Rome* Rome, Tuscany (11) and Lombardy (12) were the three 'provinces' of Italy.

11 *Ticius* presumably a Trojan founder of Tuscany, not elsewhere recorded.

12 Langobardus, legendary ancestor of the Langobardi, or Lombards, was said to be descended from Aeneas and cousin to Brutus.

13–15 Medieval authors generally accepted the foundation of Britain by Brutus, great-grandson of Aeneas, as a historical fact. They do not call him 'Felix', but the English poet Layamon regularly applies to him the epithet 'sele', meaning 'happy, fortunate'. Perhaps the *Gawain*-poet, who represents Britain as an especially grand and exciting place, is following an insular tradition of Brutus's special good fortune (cf. *with wynne* 15).

25–6 Arthur's place in the line of 'Bretayn kynges' descending from Brutus is set out in Geoffrey of Monmouth's influential *History of the Kings of Britain* (Penguin, 1966).

30 *laye* Here, as in Chaucer's *Franklin's Tale (Canterbury Tales,* V 710), a 'lay' is a shortish narrative poem concerned with marvels and adventures.

33–6 'As it is set down and fixed with a brave and powerful story, made firm with true alliteration as has long been the custom in the land.' The poet seems to claim that his lay is 'fixed' (*stad . . . stoken . . . loken*) in its present form both by the strength of its story and by the correctness of its alliterative metre. But, as often in the short lines of the quatrain ('wheel'), there are obscurities. *With lel letteres loken* may mean 'embodied in truthful words'; in which case the last line refers to the antiquity (and therefore authenticity) of the story, not to the antiquity (and therefore excellence) of the alliterative tradition.

37 Arthur held court and wore his crown (see 364) at Christmas, Easter, Ascension Day, Pentecost and All Saints (see 536).

39 The Brotherhood of the Round Table, to which Gawain and the other chief knights of Arthur's court belonged, is the special object of Morgan le Fay's test in the ensuing Adventure of the Green Chapel (see 2456–8).

43 *caroles* not 'carols' in the modern sense, but dances (usually ring-dances) accompanied by singing. The *carole* was a fashionable form of entertainment at any festivity.

60 'When New Year was so fresh that it had only just arrived', *i.e.* on New Year's Day, the eighth of the fifteen days of Christmas feasting.

64 'The clergy evidently take the lead in the shouting of "Nowell", as further amplified in the next line' (Gollancz).

66–70 Some kind of party game, perhaps a guessing game like Handy Dandy, is evidently associated with the distribution of New Year's gifts. The tone of lines 69–70 suggests that the forfeit for ladies who lost in the game was a kiss.

73   'The best man always in the most honoured position, as was most fitting'.

75–80   Guenevere sits in a baldachin, with sides of silk, a canopy above, and hangings (or carpets) of embroidered and jewelled stuffs.

79   'That could be proved of value for buying with money'.

81   *comlokest* that is, the most beautiful of the jewels, Guenevere.

87   *His lif liked him lyght* 'He liked his life to be gay' (Davis).

89   *yong blode* Of the four 'humours' it was blood which was held to predominate in young people, making them merry and active.

90   *an other maner* The fact that Arthur has not yet taken his seat is explained by reference to two distinct 'manners' or customs: his youthful habit of walking about instead of sitting down, and his noble custom of waiting for adventure before taking his seat on great feast days.

91–9   Arthur will not eat until either he hears a report of some adventure previously unheard of (*uncouthe* 93) but not incredible (*that he myght trowe* 94) or he witnesses the beginnings of a new adventure in the form of a challenge to battle.

96–9   'Or else some man craved of him some trusty knight to engage with him in jousting, a man [*lede*] to stake life against life, and each to concede the advantage to the other according as fortune chose to favour them.'

109–15   The diners are grouped in pairs, each pair sharing twelve dishes of food (128). Guenevere sits in the middle of the high table (74), on the left of the place which Arthur is to occupy, with Gawain on her left and his dining companion, Agravain, beyond him 'on the other side'. On the right of the King's place sits Bishop Baldwin, who shares dishes with Ywain. Everyone else is on lower tables or *sidbordes*.

111   Gawain and Agravain 'of the hard hand' were both sons of King Lot of Orkney. Their mother was Anna, one of Arthur's half-sisters. Morgan le Fay was another of Arthur's half-sisters, and is therefore Gawain's aunt (2464).

112   *begynnes the table* starting from the host's right, that is. The representative of the Church enjoys the place of honour.

113   *Ywan* another of Arthur's nephews, son of King Urien. *ette with himselven* 'ate with him', that is, with Baldwin.

118–20   'The fresh noise of the drums together with the noble pipes, wild and vigorous trillings, set up such a din that many a heart rose very high at their strains.'

123   *pine to finde* 'it was difficult to find'.

126   *as he loved himselve* 'as he fancied for himself'.

132–3   'Another quite new noise approached quickly, so that the man might be free to take food.' This new noise comes on top of the noise of trumpets, drums and pipes, referred to again at 134. The approach of the Green Knight, first heard here, heralds an adventure which will meet the requirements of Arthur's vow and so allow him to start eating (see 474–5).

137   'The very largest on earth in height.' *One* strengthens the superlative in this kind of expression in Middle English.

140–41   '. . . that I think he was half giant; or at any rate I reckon that he was the biggest of men . . .' The Green Knight's thick chest and massive limbs are those of a giant, but the slender waist and harmonious proportions suggest humanity and elegance (142 f.).

143   *all* 'although': 'For although his body was forbidding in back and chest . . .'.

145–6   'And all the bodily parts that he had harmonizing in shape very elegantly.' The combination of massive chest and slender waist was admired in men.

149   'He bore himself like a man who would be bold'. The meaning of *fade* is uncertain.

160   'And there the man rides with no shoes on his feet [at the bottom of his legs]'. The eye travels down the Green Knight's legs, observing his neat stockings, his gold spurs set on striped silk fabric, and finally the absence of shoes. Stockings were often worn without shoes on peaceful occasions, and the Green Knight is not dressed for war, as he later explains (271).

166   *flyes* Flying insects such as butterflies are meant.

173   'The horse that he rode on was completely of that same colour.'

186   *capados* a kind of hood and cape which covered head and shoulders: Gawain wears one under his hauberk and helmet (572). The Green Knight's beard and hair together enclose his neck and arms down to the elbows, where they are clipped off all round to give a straight edge.

187–91   The mane and also the tail and forelock of the horse are curled, combed, ornamented with knots and entwined with gold thread.

193   *as the dok lasted* The green, jewelled ribbon was wound round both tail and forelock 'as far as the cut hair lasted', that is, for their whole length.

199   'His glance was as swift as lightning' (Waldron).

206   The cluster of holly is explained later as a sign of peaceful intentions (265–6). Olive branches are more common in Arthurian romance; but holly is appropriate to the season, and it may have been used as an emblem of truce in the poet's locality.

209   'A cruel axe to describe in words, if anyone were able to.'

214   'The handle by which the grim knight gripped it was of a strong piece of wood.'

217–20   A tasselled cord is wound many times round the handle and made fast at the axe head.

222–3   Riding up to the high table without a greeting is the custom of hostile visitors in Arthurian romance.

224-7 The seat at the high table of the *governour* or presiding person is still vacant, since Arthur has not yet taken his place.

240 *fantoum* 'illusion'; *fayrye* 'magic'.

246-9 'I judge that it was not altogether from fear but somewhat from courtesy – they allowed the one to whom they were all bound to defer [Arthur] to speak to that man.' The last two lines specify the point of courtesy involved. *Bot* (248) may be a scribal mistake.

256 that is 'So help me God'.

258 f. The Green Knight's use of the singular form of address, 'thou', instead of the polite plural, 'you', is challenging to the King's dignity.

262 *other pure laykes* 'other noble sports', that is, besides the noble sport of jousting referred to in 260.

277-8 Arthur takes up the Green Knight's reference to his unarmed state: 'Even if you choose to ask for combat without armour, you will not lack adversaries here.'

287 'That dare boldly strike a single stroke in return for one other.'

290 *as bare as I sitte* 'as unarmed as you see me now.' The Green Knight is still sitting on his horse.

294-6 'And I shall stand and take one stroke from him unflinching on this floor, provided only that you will grant me the right to deal him one in return, I claim it'. *Barlay* is probably the same as the modern *barley* used by schoolboys for calling a truce and for 'bagging', but its exact meaning here is uncertain.

298 A year and a day was the period specified in law to ensure that a contract made at any time of day on, say, 1 January could be honoured at any time of day on the following 1 January.

304 *red yen* Red eyes were held to be a sign of manly courage and strength.

321 *as kene by kynde* 'as one who was by nature bold'.

331   *that strike with hit thoght* 'intending to strike with it.'

335   The *cote* is the tight-fitting coat described in 152. The Green Knight is calmly smoothing out its wrinkles.

336   *dintes* Arthur's practice swings.

346   *that* 'if'. Gawain says to Arthur: 'If you would give me the command to rise and if it would not displease my lady, I would join you'. If Gawain leaves the table, he leaves Guenevere with empty seats on both sides of her.

350   *to take hit to yourselven* 'for you to take it upon yourself', a phrase depending upon the *not semly* of 348.

355-6   'And the loss of my life would be the least, if you want to know the truth. I deserve praise only inasmuch as you are my uncle'.

360   *riche* is probably a verb meaning 'direct' (cf. 1223). Gawain asks that, if his suggestion does not commend itself, the court should simply direct matters otherwise, without blaming him for his well-meant intervention.

372-4   'Take care that you deal one stroke; and if you manage him rightly, I readily believe that you will survive the blow that he is to offer you afterwards' (Davis).

378   'Let us recapitulate the terms of our agreement before we go any further.'

384   *with no wye elles* Gawain, for obvious reasons, insists that it must be the Green Knight himself who delivers the return blow.

394 f.   This is the first intimation that the return blow will not be delivered on home ground.

412   *Bot slokes!* 'But stop!', that is, 'Enough of this talking!'

442-3   'Many a one was afraid of him by the time his speech was uttered.'

445   Bertilak later tells Gawain that one of the purposes of his mission was to frighten Guenevere (2460–62); so the 'most precious on the dais' is most likely the Queen.

447   *his mouth* 'its mouth'. *His* is the neuter as well as the masculine possessive pronoun.

454   The challenger here announces his name, as he promised earlier that he would (407–8).

465–6   The open declaration of the courtiers that the Green Knight is a *mervayl* releases Arthur from his vow not to eat, as he points out later (474–5).

471–3   'Such sport is very appropriate at Christmas, the performing of interludes with laughter and song alongside these seemly carols . . .' The carolling of the court (see 43 n) has been interrupted by a seasonable piece of mumming. Interludes were dramatic performances such as might be put on during banquets.

476–7   *gaynly* ('aptly') perhaps draws attention to Arthur's cool-headed word-play. 'Hang up your axe' was an idiomatic expression meaning 'rest from your efforts'.

480   'To describe the marvellous event with its genuine authority' (Davis). People would point to the axe as proof that there really had been a Green Knight.

491   *hanselle* Arthur's New Year's gift (cf.66) is the Adventure of the Green Chapel.

493   'Although words were lacking to him when they took their seats . . .' At the beginning of the feast Arthur had to remain standing because he had not heard either a challenge (the *yelpyng* of 492) or a report of an adventure (92–9). Both are included under *wordes*.

503   Fish and plain foods were eaten during the fast of Lent, as on the fast of Christmas Eve (888–98).

504   'But then nature's weather fights it out with winter.' Here spring struggles with winter; at 525 winter struggles with summer.

510   *somer* (here and at 516) means generally the warm part of the year. *Soft somer* is its mild phase, the spring season which begins with April showers (506).

516–17   The poet is still thinking of spring, the season of 'summer' when the mild winds blow. The reference to Zephirus, the spring breeze of Chaucer's *Canterbury Tales*, shows this. Summer in the narrower modern sense is described in 518–20.

518   *theroute* that is, out of the *sedes*.

521   'But then autumn hurries along and soon urges it [the plant] on'.

532–3   Michaelmas (29 September) marks the beginning of the last quarter of the year, and so brings a *wage*, a pledge or foretaste, of winter.

534   This line, echoing and answering 487, marks the end of the transitional passage on the seasons.

536   Gawain waits for All Saints' Day (1 November), a day when Arthur regularly held royal court (see 37 n).

541   *never the lasse ne the later* simply an expanded form of 'nevertheless'.

546–7   'You know the nature of this affair, and I am anxious not to bother you any further with the difficulties of it, or only a very little'.

551–5   Ywain, Gawain's cousin, appropriately heads this catalogue (though Gawain's brother Agravain would have been even more appropriate, see 110–11). But the rest of the list seems fairly random: Erec, hero of one of the romances of Chrétien de Troyes; Dodinal 'the wild' and his kinsman Galeshin, whom Arthur had made Duke of Clarence (cf. 678); Lancelot and his kinsman Lionel; Lucan the butler; Bors, brother of Lionel; Bedivere, brother of Lucan; and Mador the doorkeeper.

560–61   'To suffer a grievous blow and deliver none in return with his sword.'

564–5   'What can a man do with grievous and pleasant destinies except try them?'

566   *on the morn* 'on the following day', 2 November, All Souls' Day.

578–9   'Then fine thigh-pieces that closed together neatly, attached round his thick, well-knit thighs with thongs'.

586   The *cote-armure*, a tunic embroidered with the knight's heraldic device, would be worn over the hauberk or *bruny* (580) but under the sword-belt (588–9).

596   *conveyed* The members of the court accompany Gawain to the yard where he is to mount his horse.

597   *Gryngolet* commonly the name of Gawain's horse in French romance.

602   *acorded with* 'matched', that is, in colour and decoration. cf. the description of the matching ensemble of the Green Knight's horse, 168–72.

607–8   The back of the helmet is attached, presumably to the back collar of the hauberk, with a strap or *urysoun*. This ornamented strap crosses over the mail *aventayle* which is stapled round the bottom of the helmet to protect the neck and face.

611   'Parrots depicted among periwinkles'.

617–18   The 'device' of diamonds which crowns Gawain's helmet includes both kinds of diamond mentioned in the lapidaries, the clear and the brown.

620   *pentangel* The pentangle is not elsewhere given as Gawain's heraldic device. As a magical protective sign it was known from antiquity: it appears on a warrior's shield in a Greek vase-painting. Such magical properties are obviously appropriate here; but the poet was also probably aware of another, more learned tradition, according to which the figure was a symbol of perfect spiritual and physical health and well-being. This Pythagorean idea seems to lie behind the poet's exposition of the pentangle as a 'token of truth' in the following lines, for he uses the term *trauthe* very broadly to include complete moral integrity and even physical perfections.

625   The pentangle played an important part in cabbalism and came to be associated, as 'Solomon's seal', with King Solomon.

626 *by tytle that hit habbes* The pentangle symbolizes *trauthe*, not only on the authority of Solomon, but also by virtue of an intrinsic right or *tytle*, because it naturally resembles *trauthe*. The next lines explain how this is.

627 The significance of five in this context may depend upon what Sir Thomas Browne calls 'the ancient conceit [concept] of five sur-named the number of justice' (*Garden of Cyrus*, ch. 5); for *justitia* is often conceived much as the *Gawain*-poet conceives *trauthe*.

628 'And each line interlaces and joins with every other.' Each line of the pentangle touches all the other four, either by crossing or by joining at the ends.

The relevance of this in establishing the figure's 'title' to its moral signification emerges later, when the poet stresses how the various qualities which make up Gawain's *trauthe* are all similarly inter-connected (656–61).

630 *the endeles knot* cf. 657 and 660. The phrase is not recorded elsewhere.

631 f. Having established that the pentangle is a token of *trauthe*, the poet goes on to prove its fitness for Gawain by portraying his hero as a supreme exemplar of that quality.

632 Gawain was 'always true in five ways, and five times in each way'. These five pentads are expounded in the next stanza (which has 25, i.e. 5 × 5, long lines) as part of the demonstration of Gawain's *trauthe*.

636 *newe* perhaps 'newly painted'.

640 Gawain is faultless, without sin or deficiency, as far as the five senses are concerned.

641   The reference seems to be to the hero's physical prowess, exemplified by manual strength and dexterity.

642–7   The five wounds of Christ on the cross were a favourite subject of meditation and devotion, as were the five joys of Mary (Annunciation, Nativity, Resurrection, Ascension, Assumption).

653   *croked* 'out of true', a metaphor inspired by the symbolism of the pentangle.

654   *pity* 'compassion', the form which charity, the surpassing virtue, takes in knights, when they relieve damsels in distress, etc.

656–61   'Now all these five groups, in truth, were fixed in this knight, and joined each one to the other so that not one had an end, and attached at five points which never failed. Nor did they fall together on any side, or come apart either, being without a break at any angle that I can find anywhere, wherever the device may have begun or ended.' (See 628 n). In the second half of 660 it is uncertain what the author wrote: the manuscript has *jquere* in place of *I oquere*.

662   The *therfore* of this line answers the *why* of 623, which introduced the 'digression' on the pentangle.

665   *With lore* qualifying *peple*: 'people with learning'. The word 'pentangle' does not occur in earlier English texts, and was a scholarly term (Latin 'pentaculum'), in contrast to 'endless knot'.

673   *sothly* 'softly' rather than 'truly'. The *segges* are murmuring among themselves (cf. 915). The poet does not endorse their criticism of Arthur.

679–80   'He is well suited to be a brilliant leader of men here, and that would have been better than for him to be utterly destroyed'.

697–9   Having ridden out of Arthur's kingdom of Logres far into Wales, Gawain turns east along the coast road of North Wales, leaving Anglesey and its neighbouring islets on his left and fording the rivers Conwy and Clwyd.

700   *the Holy Hede* This place, where Gawain crosses the river Dee into the Wirral, is probably Holywell, a famous pilgrim centre where

St Winifred had her 'holy head' cut off and miraculously restored (cf. 2282–3). The old road across North Wales first touched the Dee near Holywell, and Gawain seems to have gone straight on over the estuary, whether by ford or in a boat. The poet writes as if he knew the area well.

701–2 'Few lived there whom either God or good-hearted men loved.' The Wirral was a forest notorious in the poet's time as a refuge for malefactors.

716 *bot ferly hit were* 'or else it was a wonder'.

738 'That she would direct him where to ride'.

750–52 'Anxious about his plight, lest he should not succeed in attending the service of that Lord who on that very night was born of a maiden to end our strife.' Such periphrases for God are characteristic of the poet (cf. 256).

762 *Cros Cryst me spede!* a common formula of prayer, with French word order ('crois Crist').

768–70 The wood is enclosed with a spiked palisade, which surrounds the castle at a radius (or to a circumference?) of more than two miles to form a *park* or game-preserve.

774 *saynt Gilyan* St Julian the Hospitaller, patron of travellers. cf. Chaucer's *House of Fame* (1022): 'Seynt Julyan, loo, bon hostel!'

776 '"Now," said the man, "I beseech you grant good lodging!"' For *bone hostel*, cf. 774 n.

778 'And he very fortunately has hit upon the main approach road'. *Gate*, 'road', is to be distinguished from *yate*, 'gate' (e.g. *yates*, 782).

785 f. Gawain has now reached the bank of the double moat, opposite the raised drawbridge. The detailed description of the castle which follows assumes that vantage-point. It starts with the outer fortifications or *barbican* (787–93), and then moves further in (*innermore* 794) to what can be seen of the rest (794–9).

791 The *garytes*, or watch-towers, form part of the outer defences, being set at intervals (*bitwene*) along the walls. They are therefore treated separately from the other towers, chimneys and pinnacles which Gawain can make out.

800–802 The pinnacles of the inner castle combine with the battlements (*carneles*) of the barbican to produce a silhouette which reminds the poet of the paper cut-outs with which dishes were decorated at medieval feasts.

813 *Peter* The porter aptly swears by St Peter, who keeps the gate of Heaven.

820 'They allowed him passage through the great gate, which was thrown wide open'.

821 *hem raysed* asked them to rise from their knees.

836–7 'Everything here is yours, for you to have at your will and bidding.' (cf. 1237–8 n.)

839 *There* used idiomatically to introduce prayers, wishes, etc.

844 *of high elde* 'in the prime of life'.

847 *fre of his speche* 'noble [*not* unrestrained] in utterance'.

849 'To exercise authority in a castle over very good men.'

853 *boure* This is the private bed-chamber assigned to Gawain for his stay.

859 The tapestries on the floor match those on the wall. The use of such expensive stuffs *under fete* is a touch of high luxury in a very luxurious passage.

864–8 'As soon as he had taken one and wrapped himself in it, one that looked well on him with its flowing skirts, truly it seemed from his appearance like springtime to almost everyone – all in colours, and all his limbs bright and beautiful underneath'. An impressionistic description; the exact meaning is in doubt.

876   *clothes* The wooden chair is covered with a quilted cloth and then with cushions, as the next line explains.

883   *his chere mended* 'his spirits rose.'

884   Tables were usually set up on trestles at this time (cf. 1648).

890   'Double portions, as is fitting [for a guest], and many kinds of fish.' The main dishes are all fish because Christmas Eve is a day of fasting, whence Gawain's compliment at 894 and the men's reply at 897.

894–6   'The knight very generously and often called it a feast with great courtesy, whereupon the men all at the same time pressed him just as courteously . . .'

898   *eft* 'afterwards', at the Christmas feast.

901–4   'Then inquiries were made of that prince in a restrained fashion by means of discreet remarks directed at him, with the result that he acknowledged courteously that he belonged to the court which the noble and gracious Arthur rules without a rival . . .'. The attendants are cautious because knights errant do not always wish to reveal their true identity; but Gawain is famed in romances for his courteous readiness to do so.

911–13   The syntax runs: 'to appear in the presence of him to whose person all excellence . . .'.

916   *slyghtes of thewes* 'examples of skilful behaviour'.

918   'We can learn, without asking, what can be achieved in conversation'.

922–3   'At a time when men rejoicing at His birth are to sit and sing'. The host later, in a similar passage, calls Christmas 'God's own feast' (1036).

926–7   'I believe that anyone who has the opportunity of listening to him will learn about love-talking.'

928   'By the time dinner was finished and the noble knight had risen from table . . .'.

934 The lady (but not the lord) enters a closed pew in the chapel.

937 'And acknowledges him in friendly fashion and calls him by his name'. The lord is represented as learning his guest's name at 908.

943–4 *fayrest in felle* (literally 'in skin') is a conventional phrase; and *of all other* belongs with it. The intervening phrases specify the fairness: of flesh, face, proportion, complexion and quality.

946 'She made her way across the chancel to entertain that gracious one.'

947–9 If this older lady were another guest in the castle, she would normally walk on her hostess's right hand side. The fact that she is on the left suggests that she is a member of the household, and *lad*, 'led', suggests a duenna. The special honour paid to her *with hatheles aboute* is therefore mysterious, until Bertilak explains it (2463 f.).

953 *that other on rolled* 'hung in folds on the other.'

956 This line probably refers not to the *kerchofes* but to the lady's breast and throat: the contrast is with the *blake* complexion of the old lady.

959–60 'Her forehead wrapped in silk and all muffled up, edged and latticed all round with ornamental details'.

968–9 'More sweet to taste was the one she had in tow.'

971 Gawain leaves the pew where he has been sitting with the lord and goes to meet the ladies.

975–6 'They desire his acquaintance, and he promptly begs to be their faithful servant, if it might please them.' Familiar expressions of 'noble talking' are here converted into indirect speech.

979 *spyces* It was customary to eat delicacies such as ginger and licorice with wine at supper.

983–7 The lord appears to challenge his guest to some kind of mock-combat, in which his hood held up high on a spear plays the part of a standard to be kept from the enemy at all costs. But the game, like those in the first fitt, is obscure.

999–1000 'Both at buffets and at regular meals elaborately prepared dishes, with doughty men arrayed on the dais in the best fashion.'

1001–2 The duenna sits in the place of honour with the master of the house (see 947–9 n).

1004–9 ... 'Right in the middle where the food fittingly came [was served first] and afterwards went through all the rest of the hall as seemed most proper. Once everyone had been duly served according to his rank, there was eating and merriment and much joy, such that it would be difficult for me to represent even if perhaps I did take pains to describe it in detail.' *And* (1009) means 'if'.

1014 *uch prynce game* 'any prince's sport'.

1023 *the last of the layk* St John's Day, 27 December, the third day of Christmas, is the last of the general feast (see 1066 n).

1025 *wonderly thay woke* 'they stayed up very late'.

1028 'Everyone who was a visitor [takes his leave] to depart.'

1029 Gawain, who intends to go next morning with the other guests, takes his leave with the rest; but the lord catches hold of him.

1035 'Indeed, sir, it will be the better with me for as long as I live'.

1045 'That he could not by any means [stay any longer].'

1053–5 '[a place] such that I do not know for the life of me where to go to find it. I would not wish to fail in arriving there on New Year's morning for all the land in Logres ...'.

1066 'I have now only three bare days to get busy in'. These are the three days of hunting and good company which occupy the following fitt. But Gawain's observation is made on the evening of 27 December, when he has in fact *four* days of the old year left. Gollancz suggested that a line lost after 1022 carried the action to 28 December; but things go by threes at Hautdesert (e.g. lines 763, 1141, 1443, 1946), and it is possible that the poet cheated in order to derive two regular groups of three days out of a period of seven.

1068 *Now leng the behoves* 'Now you must *stay*' (echoing Gawain's protestation at 1065).

1070 'Do not let the Green Chapel worry you any more'. *Upon grounde* is an alliterating tag picked up from 1058, but it suggests the idea of 'whereabouts'.

1072 *While forth dayes* 'Until well on in the day'.

1081 *Now acheved is my chaunce* 'Now that my adventure is accomplished . . .'.

1082 Gawain promises to stay (which he had previously declined to do, despite his promises of 1039–41) and do whatever else his host requires of him.

1083 *set him biside* that is, drew him down into a seat next to him.

1087 'Like a man who was going out of his mind and did not know what he would do next.'

1097 *while the messewhyle* 'until time for Mass'.

1104 'Bowing like the courteous man he was.'

1108–9 'Dear sir, let us exchange like this and answer each other honestly, to whichever man may fall the worse or the better lot.'

1112 'If someone will bring us the drink, this agreement is sealed'. The beverage which accompanies and confirms the agreement is mentioned again on the next occasion (1409). See also 1684 and 1935.

1123 'They often repeated the terms of the agreement'.

1141 *thre bare mote* The three long notes on the bugle signify the uncoupling of the hounds (cf. 1147–9).

1143 'They [the hunters] scolded and turned back those [hounds] that went chasing off'.

1147 'Huntsmen cast off leashes'.

1153   *stablye* a line of beaters who hold in the does and hinds so that the lord and his party can shoot at them.

1154–7   The close season (*fermysoun tyme*) for male deer (hart and buck) ran from September till June, whereas female deer (doe and hind) were hunted in the winter.

1162   The *broun* is the brown flesh of the deer and the *brode hedes* belong to the arrows.

1167–73   'Any wild creature which escaped the archers was pulled down and torn at the receiving stations, after being harrassed from the high ground and pursued down to the waters – the men at the lower stations were so skilled, and there were such big greyhounds which got them immediately and pulled them down as fast as men could look at them.' The deer, turned back from the high ground by beaters, are pursued downhill by small hounds (*raches* 1164) running the gauntlet of the sportsmen's bows and crossbows. Those which survive are met at the bottom of the slope by another line of stations with big greyhounds.

1174–5   'The lord, transported with delight, kept on galloping and dismounting.' He dismounts when he wants to shoot.

1182–3   'And as he slept softly on, he heard a little sound stealthily at his door and [heard it] quietly open.'

1202   'And crossed himself, as if to become the safer by his utterance.' The crossing motion would be accompanied by some such prayer as 'Cros Cryst me spede!' (see 761–2).

1210   'Now you are taken prisoner on the spot, unless a truce can be arranged between us'.

1224   'I shall fasten you down on this other side too' (cf. 1211).

1237–8   *my cors* ('my body') can mean simply 'myself' in Middle English (compare modern 'anybody'). Hence the lady can claim to be saying no more here than her husband says at 836–7, that she is entirely at the disposal of her distinguished guest: 'I am yours gladly, for you to do as you like with' (cf. also Gawain's own polite protestations,

1039, 1081, 1964). Her first remark may bear an even more innocuous sense: 'I am glad to have you here'. (So Davis, comparing the words of the Host in the *Canterbury Tales*: 'Ye been to me right welcome'.) But in any case the context renders her polite phrases highly suggestive.

1239–40 'It behoves me of very necessity to be your servant, and so I shall be.' The lady echoes and counters Gawain's remarks in 1214–16. *Servaunt* was a term of medieval love talk.

1246–7 'That I might contribute by speech or by service to the pleasure of your noble self.'

1251 *hit are* 'there are'.

1264–7 'For truly I have found in you a noble generosity, and also received a great deal besides [i.e. of generous treatment] from other people by their actions; but the honour which they bestow is never caused by my deserving – the worthiness belongs to you, who can not behave otherwise than well.' The exact sense of this piece of self-depreciation is not clear. The manuscript has *fongen her dedes* in 1265, and *nysen* for *nis ever* in 1266.

1281 'And all the time the lady behaved as if she loved him a lot'.

1283–5 'Though she were the most beautiful of women, the man was the less inclined to love on his journey because of the loss which he was going to suffer without delay'. Gawain is travelling light, emotionally as well as physically (cf. 1808 f.). In the manuscript, 1283 reads: 'Thagh I were burde bryghtest the burde in mynde hade'.

1292–3 'May He who prospers all conversation reward you for this entertainment; but it is hard to believe that you are Gawain.'

1301 'By some hint in some casual remark at some break in the conversation.'

1303–4 'I shall kiss at your command, as befits a knight; but do not continue to press your claims in this way any further lest he [the knight, i.e. Gawain himself] incur your displeasure.' Gawain implies that if the lady commands anything more than a kiss, he will be forced to refuse. *fyrre*, 'further', belongs with *plede*, as in *Pearl* 563.

1327 'And had them neatly cut open, as the operation requires.' The undoing, or breaking, of deer was conducted according to a protocol which gentlemen were expected to know.

1329 The test (*asay* 1328) of the quality of the game shows that even the skinniest deer have two fingers' breadth of fat on them – a good amount.

1330–31 The gullet (*erber*) is cut and sealed with a knot (compare 1334) to prevent the contents of the stomach spilling out during the ensuing operations.

1334 'Deftly so as not to loosen the ligature of the knot.'

1337–8 One treatise on hunting explains as follows: 'He cuts an hole between the leg and the brisket, and there puts in his knife, and looseneth the shoulder from the side . . . until he have quite taken out the shoulder, and yet left the skin of the side fair and whole.'

1340–48 This sentence describes the removal of the 'numbles', i.e. the offal running the length of the deer from the *avanters* at the front down the backbone to the haunches. The art lies in cutting this away all in one piece, *all hole* (1346).

1352 'To divide it along the backbone'.

1355 *corbeles fee* 'raven's fee'. This was a piece of gristle which by tradition was thrown up into a tree for the birds.

1358 The man who killed the deer, the man who undid it, the forester, the lord and others could all, like the raven, claim a part of the carcase – a 'fee'.

1364 To *strake* was to blow a repeated and prolonged horn-signal, such as was often used to summon the hunt together for the return home: cf. 1923 and Chaucer's *Book of the Duchess* 1312–13.

1377 'Directs his attention to the tally of very sturdy beasts', with a pun on 'tally' and 'tail'. The tails were left on the carcases.

1391 'I would yield it up [vouchsafe it] completely even if it were more.'

1393-4 'It may turn out to be the better [of our two winnings], if only you would tell me where by your own cleverness you won this same wealth.' The lord approaches the exchange in a spirit of competition, as at 1942. The value of the kiss depends on its source.

1396-7 'Since you have received what is due to you, be sure you cannot [receive] anything more.'

1407 *What newes so thay nome* 'whatever new thing they acquired'.

1409 *beverage* see 1112 n.

1412 Cocks were thought to crow the first time at midnight, then at 3 a.m., and thirdly an hour before dawn, at which time the lord gets up. He is in the field before daybreak (*see* 1415).

1419 *thornes* Boars lived among thorns and thick bushes.

1421-3 'Soon they [the hounds] give tongue at the side of a marshy thicket. The huntsman urged on the hounds which first drew attention to it [the scent], threw excited words at them with a great noise.'

1431 *In a knot* 'in a compact group' (see 1429).

1434-6 'The men cast for a scent round the crag and the marsh too, until they were quite sure that the beast which had been announced there by the bloodhounds was somewhere in them.' Finding no fresh scent round the perimeter, the huntsmen can be sure that the boar must still be hidden somewhere in the crag or the marsh. The manuscript has *knot* for *kerre* at 1434.

1438 *segges overthwert* 'across the line of men'. An example of a preposition following its object.

1440 'That had long since left the herd because of his age'. Boars were supposed to do this at the age of four years. The manuscript has: 'Long sythen for the sounder that wight for olde.'

1441-5 Manuscript damaged here; *a borelych best* is supplied in 1441.

1456-7 'But the points that stuck on his "shields" failed before their toughness, and none of the barbs would pierce his brow'. The boar standing at bay presents his tough shoulders ('shields') and bristling brows to the archers.

1474 'She was with him very early'.

1484 'And if a person teaches you how to become acquainted with them, you dismiss them from your mind.'

1490 'Wherever favour becomes apparent, to claim [a kiss] promptly'.

1494 'If I were refused, I should indeed be wrong to have offered.'

1496–7 The lady's argument is that anyone who fails to appreciate Gawain must have the dull soul of a villain, or churl, and may be treated accordingly.

1507 'Of the pains and rewards of love.'

1508–24 The main sentence, in which the lady asks why Sir Gawain of all people has failed to flirt with her, is interrupted by a long parenthesis (1512–19) on the importance of love for knights.

1509 *And yow wrathed not therwith* 'if it would not make you angry'.

1513 True love is the doctrinal essence (*lettrure*) of chivalry.

1514–16 'For to speak of the endeavours of these trusty knights, it is the inscribed title and text of their works how men have risked their lives for their true love. . . .' Knightly adventure, according to the lady, is always undertaken in the service of a mistress. The bookish metaphors of 'title' and 'text' and the bookish pun on 'works' suggest that the lady lacks Gawain's firsthand knowledge of the subject.

1526 'Ought to be keen to show to a young person. . . '.

1540–41 'But to take upon myself the task of expounding true love and treating the authentic themes and stories of chivalry. . . '.

1543 *or* 'than', in this case only.

1549–50 'Thus that noble creature put questions to him and often tried him in order to bring him to grief (whatever else she may have had in her mind).' Or *woghe* could be the verb 'woo'.

1552-3 'Nor did any evil appear on either side, nor did they feel anything but joy.'

1564-5 'Where he stood at bay, until bowmen broke it [the bay] and forced him despite himself to come further out into the open'.

1573-6 *With him then irked*. . . . 'By then all the bold men who stood round him were weary of him, of attacking him from a distance; but none dared approach him because of the danger.' Boars are included in the list of perils faced by Gawain in his journey to Hautdesert (722). They were considered very dangerous.

1585 The fierce boar (*the felle*) is at bay on a rocky ledge at the far side of a stream, at a place where the water is shallow and passable (hence *forde*).

1588 'That many were afraid for the man, lest he got the worst of it.'

1595-6 'And he with a snarl gave himself up and quickly began to float downstream.'

1607 *on high* A boar's head was customarily impaled on a stake and carried ceremoniously aloft (see 1616).

1608 'And afterwards cuts him roughly open along beside the backbone'.

1610 *rewardes* The technical term for the portion served to the dogs was 'reward'.

1613 'And further he fastens the two sides together all complete'.

1619-20 'It seemed a very long time to him until he saw Sir Gawain in the hall.'

1634 'And expressed horror at it in order to bring credit to the lord.' *Here* is an old verb meaning 'praise'.

1644 *saynt Gile* St Giles, a popular saint who lived as a hermit in the woods with a hind as a companion.

1647 'If you obtain such merchandise.' Gawain has won twice as much as on the previous day.

1655 The *coundut* was a kind of part-song (originating in the liturgy) often sung at banquets during the Christmas festivities. Fourteenth-century *coundutes* tended to adopt the stanza-and-refrain structure of *caroles* (see 43 n); so the two terms became closely allied.

1658–63 'Sweetly she directed at that man such attentions, with private, stealthy looks of favour to please the stalwart knight, that the man was quite amazed and secretly displeased; but because of his breeding he did not wish to repulse her, but behaved with complete courtesy towards her, however awry the affair went.' *wroth with himselven* probably means 'angry within himself' (Davis, comparing 2301). The last clause is obscure; but the idea seems to be that Gawain remained polite no matter how provocative the lady became.

1671 *that he to schulde* 'when he would have to arrive.' The verb of motion is omitted, according to Middle English idiom.

1678 *Chaunge with the chevisaunce* 'exchange winnings with thee'.

1680 'Now bear in mind tomorrow, "third time turn out best".' The proverb probably refers to a throw at dice.

1695–6 'The sun rises in fiery red against the cloudbank, and in full brightness skirts the clouds in the sky.'

1699–1700 'Some [hounds] hit on the scent where the fox was lurking, often trail from side to side across it as their wily practice is.' The fox keeps doubling back (see 1707) and the hounds try to catch him at it.

1703 *in his right fare* 'directly in his [the fox's] track'.

1709 *spenne* apparently some kind of hedge, at the edge of the wood from which the fox is trying to escape.

1711 'Thought to have escaped by cunning out of the wood away from the hounds.'

1719–20 'Then it was a pleasure indeed to hear the hounds, when all the pack combined together had met with him.'

1721   *sorwe* stands, by way of expressions like 'sorrow befall you', for imprecations in general.

1728   *Reynarde* The fox is several times referred to by this popular medieval name for the animal.

1730   *while mydoverunder* 'until well on in the afternoon'.

1733   *for luf* Elsewhere this phrase refers to little more than friendly sociability: 1086, 1927. It is ambiguous here.

1734   'Nor [would she allow] the purpose which was fixed in her heart to be blunted'.

1738   *houve* 'headdress', such as a married lady was expected to wear; *the hawer stones* perhaps refers specifically to pearls.

1740   The significance of a 'naked' face and throat is suggested by 954-63 above.

1752-3   'How destiny was to deal out his fate to him on the day when he meets the man at the Green Chapel'.

1756   *swares with hast* 'quickly answers' (in reply to the lady's brisk opening remarks, 1746-7).

1768-9   'There was great peril between them, if Mary be not mindful of her knight.'

1772   *lodly* 'offensively, rudely'.

1773-5   These lines explain the dilemma stated in 1772: Gawain seems obliged either to show discourtesy in refusing the lady's advances or to betray his host by accepting them.

1777-8   'With a little love-laughing he parried all the expressions of partiality which sprang from her mouth.'

1782-4   'Unless you have a mistress, someone dearer, who pleases you better, and [have your] loyalty pledged to that noble creature, attached so firmly that you do not care to loosen it - and that is what I now believe.'

1786   *for all the lufes upon live* that is, for the love of God, Christ, etc.

1788   *saynt Jon* St John the Apostle, the virgin disciple to whom Christ committed his virgin mother: and therefore appropriate for Gawain's present protestations.

1795   *mourne* a term of love-talking often applied to rejected lovers (see also 1800).

1799   *thy glove if hit were* 'even if only your glove': cf. 1807.

1805   'But to give you as a love-token something that was of little value!'

1811–12   'Every person must act according to his circumstances – do not take it amiss or hard.'

1814   *lufsum under lyne* 'lovely under linen', a traditional poetic phrase for a woman.

1817   The ring, like the *ceinture* or belt which follows, is a standard love-token in romances. Unlike Gawain, the lady is well provided with suitable gifts.

1820   The episode of the ring establishes what is later asserted more than once: that Gawain was at no time attracted by the costly nature of the lady's gifts. cf. the use of *wele* at 2037 and 2432.

1827   *to rich for hit semes* 'because it seems too costly'.

1832–3   'It was decorated with green silk and trimmed with gold, embroidered only at the edges, worked with fingers'.

1836   *nay* 'said . . . not' (past tense of *nie*, 'say no').

1856–9   'It would be a treasure for the peril which was appointed for him if he succeeded in arriving at the chapel to receive his doom. If he could escape without getting killed, it would be a noble trick. So he yielded to her insistence and allowed her to speak'.

1861   *him gafe* 'surrendered himself'.

1862   A subject 'she' is to be understood. The narrative is very rapid at this point.

1875   'Hid it very faithfully where he could find it later.' *Holdely* (cf. *lelly* at 1863) is rich with implications. Loyalty to the lady involves disloyalty to the lord.

1878   *lyste his lif* 'hear his confession'.

1880–81   'He confessed completely there and revealed his misdeeds, both greater and smaller, and asks for forgiveness'.

1884   'As if Doomsday had been fixed for the next day', that is, as if the priest knew that Gawain was to face Judgement next day – as in a sense he does.

1893   'Now let him remain in that shelter, and joy befall him.'

1901   *at the best castes* 'aims at the creature'.

1902   *schulde have arered* 'went to retreat.'

1905   *me* The same idiomatic use of the first-person pronoun to express the speaker's involvement in what he says (the 'ethic dative') is found at 1932, 2014, 2144, 2459.

1921   'And strip off his coat.' The skin is the only part they take. The contrast with the elaborate descriptions of the undoing of deer and boar suggests the contempt for the fox which the lord later expresses: 1944 f.

1923   *Strakande* see 1364 n.

1928   *blue* Gawain wears blue, the colour of faithfulness, for his single act of duplicity. The colour appears nowhere else in the poem.

1934   On the two previous occasions, the lord has been the first to yield up his winnings.

1935   *drynk* see 1112 n.

1938-41 '"By Christ," said that other knight, "you are being very fortunate in the purchase of this merchandise, if you have enjoyed favourable prices." "Oh, never mind about the prices," said the other hastily, "since the goods that I got have been openly paid over."' cf. 1395-7. For *porchas* in 1941, the manuscript has *chepes*.

1948 Gawain's '*Innogh*' is, for him, strikingly abrupt. He does not wish to discuss the matter any further.

1955-6 'Gawain and the master of the house were both as happy as could be, unless indeed the whole company had been silly or else drunk' (Cawley).

1964 'I shall give you myself in exchange for one of your men, if it please you'. Gawain politely reminds the lord of his earlier promise to assign him one of his men as a guide (see 1077).

1975-6 'The lord thanked Gawain for bringing him such honour', that is, for honouring his house with his presence. cf. 1031-4.

1985-6 *and his sere pine* . . . 'and the trouble that they had each individually taken with solicitude to serve him'.

1991 'I should not like to say whether or not he slept soundly'.

1999 *The day drives to the derk* 'the daylight comes up on the darkness' (Tolkien and Gordon).

2004 *fro the high* 'from the high ground'.

2008 see 1412 n.

2017-18 Gawain's plate armour (*paunce* and *plates*) has been well polished and his chainmail rolled (*rokked*) to get the rust off.

2021-3 'He had all his pieces of armour on, polished well and nobly, the finest knight this side of Greece'.

2025-30 'When he came to put on his noblest garment, his coat-armour with the device of pure deeds [i.e. the pentangle] worked on its velvet, gems of special power set around and attached, seams embroidered, and well lined with fine furs, yet did he not omit the belt, the lady's gift'. At 2025 the manuscript has a plural *wedes* for *wede*, as at 987.

2027 *vertuus stones* Precious stones were held to possess protective 'virtue' or power. This description of the coat-armour suggests that Gawain might have relied upon the power of the pentangle rather than that of the lady's belt.

2032 f. The sword is belted over the coat-armour (as in 586–9), and so is the love-lace.

2035 'The girdle of green silk suited that gallant well': an echo of 622, where the pentangle is in question.

2036 The green belt stands out against the red cloth, which forms the background also to the gold pentangle on Gawain's coat-armour (the *goules* of 619 and 663).

2041–2 'To suffer destruction without resistance to protect himself against sword or knife.' Gawain does not yet know which weapon his adversary will use (cf. 384).

2049 'The high-spirited horse was ready to gallop then because of his good condition'. Gryngolet is already prancing: see 2064.

2053 'The man who supports them, may he have joy!'

2059 A departing guest would normally tip household servants; but Gawain, as he has already explained to the lady, has brought nothing with him.

2061 *His schalk* the man allotted to him as guide and temporary squire by the lord.

2072–3 'Compliments the porter – he [the porter] knelt before the prince, commended him to God and wished him good day, praying that He would save Gawain'. Three forms of greeting are compressed into 2073: 'I commend you to God', 'I wish you good day' and 'God save you'.

2079 'The cloud cover was high, but it looked threatening underneath.'

2086 'At that time of the year' (Waldron.)

2096 'If you would act according to my judgement, you would fare the better for it.'

2102 *Hestor auther other* 'or Hector, or anyone else.' Hector of Troy was one of the Nine Worthies.

2109 'It seems to him as pleasant a thing to kill him as to be alive himself.'

2111 *may the knight rede* 'if the knight is able to direct affairs', i.e. if he has his way.

2121–4 'And I shall hurry back home, and I promise you further that I shall swear by God and all his good saints, so help me God and the holy relic, and enough other oaths, that I shall faithfully cover up for you. . . '.

2129 'But no matter how faithfully you concealed the matter, if I left this place. . . .'

2132 *for chaunce that may falle* 'despite anything that may happen'.

2137 *stave* 'club', a churlish weapon.

2140 f. The guide's impatient, contemptuous tone is established by his frequent use of the singular form of address, *thou*, in this speech. Previously he has always (except in 2110) used the correct *you*.

2142 'And if it pleases you to lose your life, I have no wish to stand in your way.'

2160 *gederes the rake* 'picks up the path', i.e. the path pointed out by the guide at 2144.

2167 'The clouds seemed to him to be grazed by the crags.

2170–71 'He could see no such thing in any direction, which seemed to him strange, except a kind of mound a little way off in a clearing'. *a littel on a launde* echoes a phrase from the guide's directions (2146).

2177   *and hit riches with a rogh braunch* 'and draws it tight with a rough branch' (?). The manuscript has *his riche*, perhaps for *hit riches.*

2180   The 'barrow' apparently protrudes out from the bank mentioned in 2172, and hence has only one *ende.*

2183–4   'Or a fissure in an old crag – he could not say what it was.'

2187–8   Gawain thinks of Matins, which was performed at midnight or just after, as the favourite office of this diabolic chapel.

2193   'Now I feel in all my five senses that it is the Devil. . . .'

2201   *as hit cleve schulde* 'as if it [the cliff] would split'.

2205–7   'That equipment, I believe, is being prepared in honour of meeting me, a knight, in customary fashion.' Gawain identifies the sound as that of knightly equipment being prepared for action (cf the use of *riched* at 599). *me, renk, to mete* is obscure, but seems to be a version (clumsy, because Gawain is referring to himself) of a more normal half-line illustrated in: 'Ector richit his reyne the renke for to mete' ('Hector drew his rein tight in order to meet the warrior'). *By rote,* if it means 'in customary fashion' ('by the way' has also been proposed), suggests that Gawain had been expecting something more outlandish (like the club-wielding churl of 2136–7).

2208–11   'Let God do his will. Ah well, it does not help me a bit. Even though I lose my life, no noise will make me afraid.' Perhaps *We loo!* should be understood in quotation marks, thus: 'to say "Alas!" does not help me a bit'. Otherwise Gawain may mean that thinking about providence does not help him, since God's intentions cannot be foreseen.

2215–16   'If any person wants anything, let him come here quickly, either now or never, to get his business done.'

2219–20   'Still he swished on hastily with that noise for a while and turned back to his sharpening before he would come down' (Waldron).

2223   The *denes axe,* or 'Danish axe', was a battle-axe, so called because the Vikings once favoured it.

2226 Apparently an oath by the green girdle, and as such to be attributed to Gawain, whose thoughts turn to his magic protection when he first sees the huge axe-blade. The axe in the first fitt has a 'lace' twined round its handle (217-20); but no such lace is mentioned in the case of the present axe, and it would hardly serve to measure the length of the blade, as has been suggested.

2229 Much is made in the first fitt of the fact that the Green Knight *rides* into Arthur's hall; but here he is on foot.

2230 *stele* 'handle' (*not* 'steel').

2238 'One can trust you to keep appointments.'

2239 *God the mot loke!* 'May God protect you!'

2243 'A year ago today you accepted what fell to your lot', i.e. the right to deliver the first blow.

2247 The mail *aventayle* attached to the helmet (607-8 n) would protect Gawain's neck against the blow.

2252 *Bot stightel the upon one stroke* 'Just confine yourself to a single blow. . . '.

2257-8 'And acted as if he feared nothing; he would not cower for fear.'

2263-4 'If it had come down as hard as he threatened, the man who had always been valiant [Gawain] would have died there from his blow.'

2265 *glyfte him biside* 'glanced sideways'.

2275 'Nor raised any objection in King Arthur's hall.'

2278 'Wherefore I must [*me burde*] be acknowledged the better man.'

2293-4 The double simile of the rock and the tree stump is based on the traditional alliterative coupling of 'stock' (*stubbe*) and stone.

2297–8 'May the noble order which Arthur bestowed upon you [the order of knighthood] preserve you now and protect your neck at this stroke, if it can succeed in doing so.'

2301 'I believe that your heart is afraid within you.'

2307–8 'No wonder if he found it unpleasant, having no hope of rescue.'

2310 *the barbe of the bit* 'the hooked point of the blade'. On this third occasion the Green Knight does not withhold his stroke, but lets it fall to one side of Gawain's neck, cutting him with the sharp *barbe* in the process.

2318 With a movement of his shoulders, Gawain swings his shield (which has been slung on his back) round under his left arm to confront his adversary.

2325–6 'And repay promptly, you may be sure of that – and fiercely too.'

2339–40 'No one here has mistreated you in an unmannerly fashion, nor acted towards you otherwise than as the agreement at the King's court laid down.'

2342 Bertilak's reference to other *rightes*, which he is ready to waive, can be understood only in the light of his later explanations.

2345–7 'First I threatened you in sport with an aimed blow and cut you with no gash: with justice I made you the offer [of an undelivered blow] because of the agreement we made on the first night'.

2350 *the morn* the next day after Gawain first honoured his agreement.

2354–5 'A true person must [*mon*] make true restitution; then a man need fear no danger.' The idea of *trauthe* is here identified with the medieval idea of justice as giving to each what is due to him.

2358 *my wede* not because it once belonged to his wife, but because it should justly be his under the Exchange of Winnings agreement.

2362-3 'I sent her to try you – truly, it seems to me, quite the most faultless man that ever trod ground.' See 137 n.

2364 'As a pearl by comparison with the white pea is of greater value'.

2367 *wylde werk* 'skilful workmanship'. The elaborate workmanship of the girdle is emphasized also at 2037-9 and 2430-2.

2374 *covetyse* Gawain three times accuses himself of covetousness (cf. 2380 and 2508); yet we are also specifically told that he did *not* desire the girdle for its richness and fine workmanship (2037-9, 2367, 2430-2). However, the act of withholding something justly due to another person was classed among the acts of covetousness in medieval manuals; and this is what Gawain did when he hid the girdle from Bertilak.

2381 *largesse* and *lewty* are the exact and formal opposites of *covetyse* and *trecherye* (or *untrauthe,* 2383) respectively.

2387 'Let me regain your goodwill' *or* 'Let me understand your will'.

2396-9 'Because it is as green as my gown, Sir Gawain, you can be reminded of this same contest when you make your way among noble princes; and this will be an excellent token of the Adventure of the Green Chapel among chivalrous knights.'

2400 'And you must come back on this New Year's Day to my house'.

2409 *I have sojourned sadly* 'I have stayed with you long enough'.

2416-19 The list of great men ruined by women, as Adam was ruined by Eve, is conventional in medieval writing.

2419 *that much bale tholed* This refers to David's penance after the death of Bathsheba's husband (II Samuel 12).

2420-24 'Since these were afflicted through their wiles, it would be a great advantage to love them well and trust them not at all, if a man could. For these were the noblest of former times, and every prosperity attended them pre-eminently above all others who lived under the heavens.' *mused* is literally 'thought'.

2428 'It seems to me that I should be excused.'

2439 'But there is one thing I should like to ask you – do not be displeased'.

2443 *right name* Gawain's adversary earlier announced himself as 'the Knight of the Green Chapel' (454). Gawain now wants to know his true, everyday name.

2445 *Hautdesert* is the name of Bertilak's regular dwelling-place, that is, the castle where Gawain spent Christmas. It means 'high and lonely place'.

2446–51 An obscure passage. The second half of 2448 reads 'mony ho taken' in the manuscript, which does not make sense. If *ho* is changed to *has,* the sentence runs: 'Through the agency of Morgan le Fay, who dwells in my house, and through learned skills well and artfully mastered, many people have experienced the magic powers of Merlin; for she formerly had a very intimate love-affair with that excellent scholar, as all your knights at home know.' Morgan, that is, mastered the learned skills of her lover; and so, through her agency, Merlin's magic came to be exercised on people like Bertilak.

2460 Morgan's hatred of Guenevere is explained in other romances by a story of how the Queen frustrated her in a love-affair.

2464 see 111 n.

2465–6 Morgan, like Gawain's mother, was daughter of the Duchess of Tintagel, who afterwards became the mother of Arthur by King Uther Pendragon.

2469–70 'And I wish you as well, sir, by my faith, as any man on earth, because of your great integrity.' Bertilak places his last emphasis on *trauthe,* the quality symbolized by Gawain's pentangle (626 and n).

2471 'And he said no to him, he would by no means [accept the invitation].'

2488 The girdle is a 'token' of Gawain's fault primarily because of the manner in which he acquired it; but it also resembles the ropes worn as halters round the neck by penitents. Notice, too, the mention of the left, or evil, side in the preceding line.

2490 *the grete* 'the great ones', the nobles.

2506 A *bende* was a ceremonial sash, and also a heraldic device: a band running diagonally from top right to bottom left (cf 2487) of the shield. The *blame*, or reproach, which he 'carries in his neck' is the scar.

2508 *covetyse see* 2374 n.

2510 'And I must of necessity wear it for as long as I live.'

2511–12 The meaning of Gawain's final pronouncement is uncertain. Perhaps: 'For no-one can conceal his guilt without misfortune befalling; for where it once becomes fixed it will never be separated.' Gawain had concealed his guilt even from himself, and now he suffers the misfortune (*unhap*) of wearing a 'token of untruth' for the rest of his days. But Davis, emending *none* (MS *non*) to *mon* and taking *unhap* as a verb and *hitte* (MS *hit*) as the pronoun 'it', translates: 'For a man may hide his (spiritual) harm, but cannot unfasten (get rid of) it.'

2515 The manuscript has 'lordes and ladis'; but it is most irregular for ladies to be enrolled in the Brotherhood, and *burn* in the next line suggests that only men are in question. Probably the poet wrote *lordes and ledes* (cf. 38).

2518 'And wear that to match [Gawain's] for that man's sake.'

2523 *Brutus bokes* 'chronicles of Britain'. On Brutus, see 13–15 n.

2524–8 'Since the time when Brutus, the bold man, first came here, after the siege and the assault had finished at Troy, certainly many adventures such as this have occurred here in times past.' cf. the opening of the poem, and also 23–4.

HONY SOYT . . . The presence of this, the motto of the order of the Garter, at the end of the text suggests that the closing episode of the poem might represent the founding of a new chivalric order. However, the Arthurian order of the Green Lace, if such it is, does not correspond in detail to the English order of the Garter or to any other fourteenth-century order.

Manuscript Readings

Below are listed all the places where the reading of the one surviving manuscript, MS. Cotton Nero A. x in the British Museum, differs significantly from that given in the present text. The reading of the present text is given first, inside the square bracket.

   77 and *supplied*
  144 Both] bot
  162 *second* the] other
  210 lenkthe . . . hed] hede . . . lenkthe
  236 glowande] lowande
  343 Wawayn] Gawan
  438 he were] ho we
  531 fage] sage
  591 auther] over
  660 I oquere] jquere
  726 nas] was
  777 gyrdes] gederes
  795 Towres] towre
  815 yerne and come *supplied*
  835 wone] welde
  884 table] tapit
  893 sawses] sawes
  946 Ho] he
  958 chalk] mylk
  967 balwe] bay
  971 lent] went
  987 wede] wedes
  992 lord] kyng
 1014 That] and
 1032 that] and
 1053 ne *supplied*
 1137 By than that] By that that
 1183 dernly] derfly

1208 gay] fayr
1265 by *supplied*
1266 nis ever] nysen
1281 as him] ahym
1283 ho] I
　　　burn] burde
1293 not *supplied*
1334 *first* the] and
1345 Evendoun] evenden
1386 That] and
　　　wonnen *supplied*
1389 he] ho
1406 What] that
1434 kerre] knot
1440 fro] for
　　　seyed] wight
1441 a borelych best *supplied*; *manuscript illegible*
1442-5 *first parts of lines damaged*
1473 To com] com to
1485 taght the] taghtte
1580 and *supplied*
1588 freke] frekes
1595 yede doun] yedoun
1623 laghter] laghed
1639 hent *supplied*
1700 traveres] trayteres
1719 list upon live] lif upon list
1738 houve] hwes
1752 dele him *supplied*
1755 come *supplied*
1770 prynces] prynce
1815 nad] hade
1825 swyftly] swyftel
1863 fro] for
1878 lyste] lyfte
1893 let *supplied*
1906 laches him] caches by
1936 the *supplied*
1941 porchas] chepes
2025 wede] wedes
2053 he] thay
2105 dynges] dynnes

2177 hit riches] his riche
2187 Here] he
2205 as] at
2319 bronde] sworde
2329 Festned in *supplied*; *manuscript illegible*
2337 ryngande] rykande
2448 has] ho
2461 gome] gomen
2472 bikennen *supplied*
2482 he] and
2506 in *supplied*
2515 ledes] ladis

Glossary

abataylment n. battlement
abelef adv. slantwise
abloy adj. transported
abode n. delay
aboute adv. and prep. about, round
above adv. above; in a higher place 73; in the highest place 112
achaufe v. warm
acheve v. achieve; *acheve to* reach
acole v. embrace
acorde v. agree; reconcile; *acorde me with* come to terms with; *acorde with* match
after prep. after; along 218
afyaunce n. trust
aghlich adj. fearsome
aghte past tense of oghe possess, owe
Agravayn a la dure mayn Agravain 'of the hard hand'
agreve v. overcome
alder n. prince 95
algate adv. at any rate
all adv. altogether 246, etc.; *conj.* although 143
All Hal Day All Saints' Day (1 November)
aloft prep. upon 1648
alose v. praise
als adv. also
alther intensive prefix in superlatives (greatest, etc.) of all
alvisch adj. elvish, supernatural
anamayl v. enamel
and conj. and; if 1009, 1245, 1271, 1393, etc.
anele v. pursue
angard n. arrogance
anger n. harm
anious adj. troublesome
anyskynnes adj. of any kind

apende v. appertain, be fitting
apert adj. exposed to view, open
apparayl n. ornamentation
are adv. previously
arere v. run back
arounde adv. at the edges
arsouns n. saddle-bows
arwe adj. afraid
arwe v. be afraid
asay n. 'assay', test of the quality of game
ascrye v. shout
askes n. ashes 2
asoyle v. absolve
as-swythe adv. at once
as-tit adv. at once
athel adj. noble
attle v. intend; threaten 2263
atwape v. escape
aumayl n. enamel
auncian adj. aged; *as n.* aged person
aunter n. adventure
aunter v. venture
auther adv. and conj. either; or; else 1956, 2293
avanters n. front part of 'numbles' 1340–48 n
ave n. the Ave Maria, 'Hail Mary'
aventayle n. mail neck-guard attached round the bottom of the
  helmet
avinant adj. pleasant
avyse v. devise; look at 771
awharf v. past tense turned back
awles adj. fearless
ayayn adv. back, in return, again
ayayn(es) prep. against, towards
ayther adj. and pron. each; *ayther . . . other* each . . . the other
aywhere adv. everywhere

bale n. destruction, misery
balwe adj. swelling
baly n. belly
barbe n. barb (of arrow) 1457; point (of blade) 2310
barbican n. outer fortification
bare adj. bare, simple; single 1141; without armour 277, 290;
  adv. barely; openly 465

barely adv. without more ado
baret n. strife
barlay (?) I claim it, 'bags I'
barre v. decorate with bars or stripes
Barsabe Bathsheba
bastel n. castle tower (*bastille*)
bate n. (?) baiting
bauderyk n. baldric, strap (for shield, etc.) worn diagonally across the
  body
Bawdewyn Baldwin
bawemen n. bowmen, archers
bay n. bay; *bide (at) the bay, bide in his bay* stand at bay
baye v. bay, bark at
bayn adj. obedient
bayst v. *past tense* was dismayed
baythe v. grant, consent
beau adj. fair (sir)
becom v. (*past tense become*) become; go 460
bede v. (*past tense bede*) offer; command
beforne adv. previously
begyn v. begin; *begynnes the table* has the place of honour
beholde(n) past participle obliged; in duty bound 1547
behove v. (*impersonal*) behove; *the behoves* it behoves thee, etc.
beknow v. acknowledge, confess
helde n. boldness
bele adj. gracious; *bele chere* gracious company
bende n. sash, heraldic device 2506 n.
bende v. *past tense* bent, arched 305; *past participle* brought about
  2115; curved 2224
bene adj. pleasing; *adv.* pleasantly
bent n. field, battlefield; land 1599
bent-felde n. field
berdles adj. beardless
bere v. (*past tense bere*) bear; *bere on him* pressed on him 1860
berwe n. barrow, mound
best n. beast
beten past participle set 78, 2028; embroidered 1833
bette past participle kindled
beverage n. drink (sealing a bargain)
bever-hewed adj. beaver-coloured, reddish brown
bide v. (*past tense bode*) remain, await; suffer; survive 374

big adj. strong
bigge v. build, found
bigly adv. mightily
bigog interj. by God
bihinde adv. behind; inferior 1942
bikenne v. commend
bilive adv. quickly
biseme v. suit, be fitting (for)
biside prep. beside; *him biside* sideways 2265; *adv.* alongside, round
  about
bisides adv. at the sides, round about
bit n. cutting edge, blade
bitidde past tense of bityde befall
bitwene adv. at intervals 791, 795
blande n. mingling; *in blande* mingled
blande past participle trimmed
blasoun n. shield
blaunner n. kind of fur, (?) ermine
bleaunt n. kind of rich material 879; mantle made of it 1928
blenche v. start back
blend v. blind, delude
blenk v. glisten
blent v. past tense and past participle mingled
blesse v. say 'God bless you' to 1296; *blessed him* crossed himself
  2071
blonk n. horse
blowe v. bloom 512
blubred v. past tense bubbled
bluk n. trunk, headless body
blunder n. trouble
blusch n. gleam
blusch v. glance, look; gleam
blykke v. gleam
blynne v. cease
bobbaunce n. pomp
bobbe n. cluster
bode n. bidding 852; offer 1824
bode past tense of bide wait
boden past participle of bid ask
bole n. tree-trunk
bolne v. swell
bonchef n. happiness

bone n. boon, request

bone adj. in *bone hostel* good lodging

bonk n. bank, hillside; *have bonk* reach the shore 700

Boos Bors

bor n. boar

borde n. band, strip of cloth 159, 610

borelych adj. massive

borne n. burn, stream

bost n. clamour

bot adv. only, but 30, 280, 356, etc.; *bot oure one* quite by ourselves 1230; *conj.* except; unless 716, 1210, etc.

bote past tense of bite

boun adj. ready; *boun to* bound for 548

bounden past participle bound, attached; trimmed, adorned 573, 600, 609

bounty n. goodness, virtue

bourde n. jest

bourde v. jest

boure n. bower; bedchamber 853

bout prep. without

bowe v. turn, go, come

brace n. pair of arm-pieces

brach (et) n. hound

brad past participle grilled

bradde v. past tense reached

brath adj. fierce

brathly adv. fiercely

brawne n. boar's flesh; *such a brawne of a best* so much flesh on a boar

brayde v. draw, pull; spurt 429; turn 440; swing 621; throw 2377; *past participle brayden* embroidered 177, 220, 1833; linked 580

braye v. cry out

brayn adj. (?) rash

braynwod adj. frenzied

bredes n. planks (of the drawbridge)

brek(en) v. past tense broke; cut open 1333; broke down 1564; broke out 1764

breme adj. vigorous, fierce, wild; *adv.* stoutly 781

bremely adv. vigorously, fiercely, quickly

brenne v. burn

brent adj. steep 2165

brent past participle of brenne burn; *brent gold* gold refined by fire

bresed adj. bristling
brether n. plural of brother
breve v. declare, announce
britten v. break up, destroy, cut up
broke n. stream
bronde n. sword; burnt piece of wood 2
broun adj. brown 618, 879; bright 426; *the broun* the brown flesh
    1162
bruny n. shirt of mail, hauberk
brusten past participle burst, split
Brutus Trojan founder of Britain; *Brutus bokes* chronicles of Britain
brygge n. drawbridge
brymme n. water's edge
bult past tense of bylde build, dwell
bur n. onslaught, blow; force 2261
burde n. damsel, maiden, lady
burde v. (impersonal) me burde I ought to
burgh n. city, castle
burn n. man
burnyst past participle polished
busk n. bush
busk v. get ready; array; hurry, offer 2248
busy v. get busy 1066; stir up 89
busynes n. importunity 1840; solicitude 1986
by conj. (also *by that* and *by than that*) by the time that 443, 928,
    1006, 1137, 1169, 1321, etc.
Bydver Bedivere
byght n. fork (of legs)

cach v. (past tense caght) take, seize; *caght to* laid hold of; get,
    receive; urge on 1581, 2175; go 1794
cacher n. huntsman
calle v. call, shout, cry; *calle . . . of* beg for 975, 1882
capados n. a kind of hood
caple n. horse
carneles n. battlements
carole n. dance-song
carp n. speech
carp v. speak, tell
case n. case, affair; chance 907; *uch a case* everything that chanced
    1262

cast n. utterance 1295; stroke 2298; fastening 2376; trick 2413

cast v. cast, throw; utter, speak 64, 249; consider 1855; aim 1901; make 2242, 2275

cavelacioun n. trivial argument 683; objection 2275

cayre v. ride

cemme v. comb

cercle n. circlet on helmet

chace n. hunt

chaffer n. merchandise

charge n. importance; *no charge of* it does not matter about 1940

charge v. charge; put on 863

chargeaunt adj. onerous

charre v. turn back, return; *him charred* went off 850

charres n. business

chaunce n. chance, fortune; adventure 1081, 1838, 2399, 2496

chauncely adv. fortunately

chaunge v. change; exchange

chauntry n. chanting (of Mass)

chefly adv. quickly

chek n. fortune; misfortune

chepe n. price

chepe v. bargain, go shopping

chere n. facial expression; *chaunge chere* look this way and that 711, 2169; behaviour, cheer; spirits 883; *bele chere* gracious company 1034

cheryse v. entertain

ches past tense of *chose*

cheve v. acquire; bring about 2103; come 63, 1674

chevisaunce n. winnings, merchandise; purchase 1939

childgered adj. boyish

chose v. choose; pick out, perceive 798; make one's way (also *chose the gate, chose the way*) 451, 778, 930, 946, 1876; undertake 1838

chymble v. wrap up

chymny n. fireplace; chimney 798

chyne n. chine, backbone

clamber v. cluster

clanly adv. cleanly, completely

clannes n. purity

clene adv. cleanly; neatly, elegantly 146, 792; completely 1298, 2391

clenge v. cling; *clenge adoun* (?) shrink down

clepe v. call

clere adj. clear, bright, beautiful; *as n.* beautiful lady 1489

clergye n. learning

clerk n. scholar

cleve v. split

clomben v. past tense climbed

close v. close, enclose; *closed fro* shut off from 1013

closet n. closed pew

cloyster n. enclosure

cofly adv. promptly

cogh v. cough, clear one's throat

cole v. cool, relieve

com v. (past tense come) come

comaunde v. command; commend 2411

comly adj. beautiful, noble; *adv.* graciously

compas n. form, proportion

compast v. past tense pondered

con v. (1) *(past tense couth)* can, be able; *noght bot wel connes* cannot behave otherwise than well 1267

con v. (2) *past tense auxiliary + infinitive* did

conable adj. excellent

concience n. mind

convey v. escort

conysaunce n. heraldic device

coproun n. ornamental top

corbel n. raven 1355 n.

cors n. body; *my cors* myself 1237 n.

cortayn n. curtain (round a bed)

corven past participle carven

cosse n. kiss

cost n. nature, quality; *costes* condition, plight 750; customs 1483; *costes of care* (?) hardships

coste v. coast, skirt 1696

cote n. coat, tunic; coat-armour 637, 2026

cote-armure n. coat-armour, tunic worn over the hauberk and embroidered with a heraldic device

coundue v. conduct

coundutes n. part-songs

counsel n. advice; *to your counsel* to advise you

countenaunce n. custom 100; expression 335; favour 1490, 1539; looks of favour 1659

couple v. leash (in pairs)

couples n. leashes

court-feres n. companions at court

couth past tense of con v. (1) can

couthe adj. evident
couthly adv. familiarly
covertour n. caparison, covering for horse 602; coverlet 855, 1181
covetyse n. covetousness
cowters n. elbow-pieces
crabbed adj. harsh 502; perverse 2435
craft n. art; skill; sport
crakkyng n. blaring
crathayn n. churl
crave v. crave; claim 1384
cresped past participle curled
crevisse n. fissure
croked adj. crooked
cropure n. crupper
croun n. top of the head 419, 616
curious adj. skilfully worked

dalt(en) past tense and past participle of dele deal
daly v. make polite conversation
dalyaunce n. polite conversation
Dalyda Delilah
dare v. cower
Davyth King David
dawed v. past tense was worth
daynty n. courtesy, honour; *had daynty* [. . .] *of* was admired 1889;
    dayntyes delights, delicacies
daynty adj. delightful
debate n. strife, resistance
debate v. dispute
debonerty n. courtesy
dece n. dais
defende v. defend; *past participle* forbidden 1156
dele v. deal; give; (?) converse 1668; receive 1968
deliver adj. quick
deliverly adv. quickly
delyver v. deliver; assign 851
deme v. judge, assess; agree
denes adj. Danish
depart v. separate; depart
departyng n. separation
depaynt(ed) past participle depicted
deprece v. release

deprese v. subjugate 6; press 1770
dere adj. dear, precious, fine, noble; festive 92, 1047; pleasant 564;
   as derrest myght falle in the noblest fashion possible 483
dere v. harm
derely adv. courteously, nobly; neatly 1327; deeply 1842
derf adj. strong; grievous 564, 1047
derfly adv. boldly
derne adj. secret, private
dernly adv. quietly, stealthily
derworthly adv. honourably
devaye v. refuse
deve v. strike down
devise v. relate
devys n. device, piece of ornamental workmanship
deye v. die
dight v. set; appoint; prepare; *dight me the dome* grant me the right
   295; *him dight* went 994
dille adj. stupid
dint n. blow
discover v. reveal
disert n. desert, merit
disport n. entertainment
dispoyl v. strip
dit past participle fastened
do v. do; *drede dos me* makes me afraid 2211; *didden hem undo* caused
   them to be cut up 1327; put 478; *do way* put aside 1492; *dos hir*
   makes her way 1308; *dos go on!* 1533
Doddinaual de Savage Dodinal 'the Wild'
doel n. lamentation
doelful adj. grievous, lamentable
dok n. cut hair (of tail and forelock)
dole n. part
dome n. judgement, doom
donkande present participle moistening
doser n. wall tapestry
dote v. lose one's wits; *doted* out of their mind 1151
doublefelde adv. with double helpings
doute n. fear
douth n. company
dowelle v. dwell, remain
draght n. drawbridge
dravel v. mutter

drawe v. draw; obtain 1647
drech n. delay
drepe v. kill
dresse v. array, prepare; direct 445; proceed 474; *dressed to* on their
  way to 1415; *dressed up* got up 2009
drive v. drive; deliver (blow); pass (time); make 558, 1020; come
  121, 222; *drive to* enclose 786, come up on 1999
droupyng n. troubled sleep
drow(en) past tense of drawe
drury n. love; *dalt drury* had a love affair; love-token
drye adj. resolute; incessant 1460; heavy 1750; *drawe on drye* detain;
  adv. strongly
drye v. endure, survive
Dryghtyn n. the Lord God
dryly adv. unceasingly
dubbe v. adorn, array
dut n. joy
dutte v. past tense feared
dyng v. strike
dyngne adj. worthy

eft adv. again, afterwards
eft(er)sones adv. again
egge n. edge (of the axe-blade); weapon 2392
eke adv. also
elde n. age, generation; *of high elde* in the prime of life
elles adv. else; in other things 1082; *conj.* provided only that 295
elnyerde n. ell (45 inches)
em n. maternal uncle
enbaned past participle provided with horizontal coursings
enbelyse v. adorn, embellish
enbrawded past participle embroidered; also *enbrawden*
enclyne v. bow
endite v. do (to death)
enfouble v. muffle up
enker adv. (?) bright
Ennias Aeneas
ennourned past participle adorned; ornamentally worked 2027
enquest n. inquiry
entayled past participle depicted
enterlude n. dramatic entertainment, mumming
entyse v. attract

erande n. mission, message
erbe n. plant
erber n. gullet
erde n. earth; land
etayn n. giant, ogre
ethe adj. easy
ethe v. conjure, pray
even adv. just, right; *on . . . even* straight at 1589; *in . . . even* straight
   into 1593
evendoun adv. right down
eves n. edge, border
evesed past participle clipped
exellently adv. preeminently
expoun v. describe, utter, expound

fade adj. (?) bold; (?) hostile
fage n. deceit; *no fage* in truth
falce adj. false, untrue
fale adj. pale
falle v. fall; happen; fall to one's lot 2243, 2327; befit 358, 890, 1303,
   1358
falssyng n. breaking of faith
fannand present participle fanning, (?) spreading out like a fan
fantoum n. illusion
farand adj. splendid
fare n. conduct; doings 409, 2494; feast 537; entertainment 694;
   track 1703
fare v. (past tense ferde) go; behave; *ferde with defence* was on the
   defensive
fast adj. firm, binding; *adv.* vigorously, quickly
faut n. fault
fautlest adj. superlative most faultless
fawne v. stroke
fax n. hair
fay n. faith; *ma fay* by my faith
fayn adj. pleased
fayntyse n. treacherousness
fayrer adj. comparative fairer; *the fayrer* the advantage 99
fayrye n. magic
faythely adv. truly
fech v. fetch, obtain
fee n. perquisite; *corbeles fee* raven's fee 1355 n.; payment

feersly adv. proudly; fiercely
felawe n. companion
felawschip n. comradeship
felde v. fold
fele adj. many; *feler comparative* more
felefolde adj. manifold
felle n. skin; fur
felle adj. fierce; *the felle* the fierce creature 1585
felly adv. fiercely
feme v. foam
fer adv. far; *comparative fyrre* further
ferde n. fear 2130, 2272
ferde v. past tense and past participle feared; afraid
ferde(n) past tense of fare
fere n. (1) company; *in fere* with a force of warriors (?) 267
fere n. (2) companion; equal; wife 2411
fere adj. proud
ferk v. go, ride; *ferkes him up* gets up
ferly adj. wonderful; *as n.* a wonder; *adv.* wonderfully
ferlyly adv. wonderfully
fermysoun n. close season
fest n. feast, festival
fest v. past tense made fast
festned past participle made fast
fete v. act
fetled past participle fixed
fetly adv. deftly
fette past participle of fech fetch
fetures n. parts of the body
feye adj. doomed to death
fildore n. gold thread *(fil d'or)*
first adj. first; *(up)on first* at the beginning; first
flagh past tense of fle and flye
flat n. plain
fle v. (past tense flagh and fled) flee; flinch 2272, 2274, 2276 (second *flagh* of line)
fiet n. floor (of hall or chamber)
flete v. (past participle floten) fleet, speed; travel 714
flode n. sea, stream
flone n. arrow
flosche n. pool
floten past participle of flete travel

flye n. flying insect
flye v. (past tense flagh) fly
fnast(ed) v. past tense snorted, panted
foch v. receive; take
folde n. land; earth
folde v. (past participle folden) enfold; *folde to* belong to 359,
  match 499; plait 189; go 1363; plight, pledge 1783
fole n. (1) horse, charger (*not* foal)
fole n. (2) fool 2414
folwe v. follow; *present participle folwande* matching
fonde v. try out; try
fonde v. past subjunctive of finde find 1875; *also past indicative*
fonge v. (past tense fong, past participle fong, fongen) receive; take
foo adj. forbidding; *adv.* fiercely 2326
for conj. for; because 258, 271, etc.
for prep. for; for fear of 1334; before 965
forbe prep. beyond
force n. force; necessity 1239
forfaren past participle killed
forferde v. past tense killed
forfete v. transgress
forlond n. headland
forme n. manner; shape
forme adj. first; *the forme* the beginning
forne adv. in former times
forsake v. deny, refuse; forsake
forsnes n. fortitude
forst n. frost
forth adv. forth; *forth dayes* well on in the day 1072
forthy adv. for this reason, therefore, wherefore
forw n. channel
forward n. agreement
forwondered past participle amazed
foryate v. past tense forgot
foryelde v. repay, reward
foryeten past participle forgotten
fotte v. fetch, get
founde v. hasten; set out 267
fourches n. legs
foyn v. thrust at
foysoun n. abundance
fraunchyse n. generosity, magnanimity

frayn v. ask; put questions to 1549; seek out 489

frayst v. ask; *frayst my fare* call and ask how I am getting on 409;
seek; test 503, 1679

fre adj. noble

freke n. man, knight

frely adv. generously, readily

fremedly adv. as a stranger

French flode English Channel

frenge n. fringe

Frenkysch adj. French; *Frenkysch fare* French behaviour (i.e.
elaborate politeness)

fres v. past tense froze

fresch adj. fresh; *the fresch* fresh food

freschly adv. eagerly

fro conj. after 8, 62

frote v. rub

frounse v. crease

frount n. forehead

fryth n. woodland

fulsun v. favour

fust n. fist, hand

fute n. trail, scent

fyche v. fix, attach

fye v. match, go well together

fyke v. flinch

fyle v. sharpen

fylle v. fulfil

fylor n. sharpening tool

fylter v. contend

fylyoles n. pinnacles

fyne adj. perfect, complete; *of fyne force* of very necessity;
adv. completely

fynger n. finger, finger's breadth (as unit of measurement)

fynisment n. conclusion

fynly adv. completely

fyrre adv. comparative further; moreover

fyske v. scamper

game n. game, jollity, pleasure; quarry 1635; process, device 661

gard v. past tense caused

gargulun n. throat

garysoun n. treasure; keepsake 1807

garyte n. watch-tower

gast adj. afraid

gate n. way, road; *chef gate* main approach road; *have the gate* have free passage

gaudi n. (?) ornamentation, (?) brightness

gayn adj. prompt, obedient; good 1241, 2491; *at the gaynest* by the most direct way; adv. promptly

gayn v. be of use to

gaynly adv. aptly 476; rightly 1297

geder v. gather, lift; pick up 2160

gentyle adj. noble, gracious

gere n. gear, equipment 569, 584, 2205; *plural* bedclothes 1470

gere v. dress; decorate; array 791

get n. winnings

gif v. *(past tense gafe, past participle geven)* give; wish (good day); *him gafe* surrendered himself 1861

Gile St Giles

Gilyan St Julian the Hospitaller

giserne n. axe

glam n. din

glaum n. din

glaver n. babble

gle n. merriment; delight

glede n. red hot coal

glemer v. gleam

glent n. glance

glent v. *past tense* glanced 82, 476; glinted 172, 569, 604, 2039; sprang 1652; flinched 2292

glod v. *past tense of glyde* glide, come

glode n. (?) patch; *on glode* (?) on the ground 2266

glopnyng n. dismay

glyfte v. *past tense* glanced

glyght v. *past tense* glanced

goande present participle of go walking (i.e. dismounted) 2214

gome n. man

gomenly adv. merrily

good n. goodness; advantage; property 1064

good-mon n. master of the house

gorger n. neckerchief

gost n. soul

gostlych adv. uncannily

goules n. gules, red (in heraldry)

grame n. mortification
grant merci many thanks
grattest adj. *superlative* greatest; thickest
grayn n. blade (of an axe)
grayth adj. ready
graythe v. prepare, dress, array; set 74, 109
graythly adv. promptly; duly
grece n. fat; flesh
greme n. wrath, grief, hurt, mortification
grenne v. grin
gres n. grass
gret v. *past tense* greeted
grete v. weep
greve n. grove
greves n. greaves, armour for the leg below the knee
grome n. man, servant
gronyed v. *past tense* grunted
gruch v. bear ill will; *present participle gruchyng* with displeasure
grue n. grain, whit
grye v. (?) shudder
gryndel adj. fierce
gryndellayk n. ferocity
gryndelly adv. fiercely
gryndelston n. grindstone
Guenore Guenevere
gurde past participle girt
gyng n. company
gyrde v. strike (spurs)

haded past participle beheaded
halche v. embrace; enclose 185; twine 218; join 657, 1613; wrap 1852
hale v. draw 1338; rush 136, 458; pass 1049; rise 788; shoot 1455
half n. side
halme n. shaft, handle
halowe v. shout (at)
halse n. neck
halve n. *oblique case of half* side; *(up)on Goddes halve* for God's sake
halwe n. saint
halydam n. holy relic
hame n. home
han present plural of have
hande n. *(honde at* 490) hand; *out of hande* straight away 2285

hanselle n. New Year's gift
hap n. happiness
hapnest adj. superlative most fortunate
happe v. fasten, clasp
harden v. urge on
hardily adv. assuredly
hardy adj. brave
harled past participle tangled
harme n. injury; guilt 2511
harnays n. harness, equipment
harnayst past participle clad in armour
haspe n. fastening
haspe v. clasp; attach
hastlettes n. entrails
hat v. be called
hathel n. man; being (God) 2056
hauberghe n. hauberk, shirt of mail
Hautdesert 'high, solitary place' (Bertilak's castle)
haviloun v. double back
hawer adj. ready 352; (?) goodly 1738
hawtesse n. pride
haylse v. greet
hedles adj. headless
hef past tense of heve lift
helde v. proceed, follow 221, 1523, 1692, 1922; bow 972, 1104;
     sink (in the west) 1321; move 2331
helder adv. rather; *never the helder* never the more (for that) 376,
     430
hem pron. them
heme adj. becoming
hemely adv. becomingly
hende adj. courteous, gracious, noble; *adv.* courteously
hendelayk n. courtesy
hendly adv. courteously
heng v. hang
henne adv. hence
hent v. (past tense and past participle hent) take, receive, catch
her pron. their
herber n. lodging
herber v. lodge
here n. (1) company of warriors 59, 2271
here n. (2) hair

here v. praise, bring credit to 1634
heredmen n. retainers
herken v. hear; hear tell of 1274; listen
herle n. thread
herre adj. comparative higher
hersum adj. devout
hervest n. harvest time, autumn
hes n. promise
hest n. command
Hestor Hector of Troy
hete n. promise
hete v. promise
hethen adv. hence
hetterly adv. vigorously, suddenly, fiercely
hette past tense and past participle of hete promise
heve v. lift
heven v. raise
hevenryche n. kingdom of heaven
hevy adj. heavy; grievous, serious 496
hewe n. hue, colour
hewe v. cut; hammer (gold) 211
hider adv. hither
high adj. high; *the high* the high ground 1152, 1169, 2004; *(up)on high* on high, to the highest degree 48; loud; *on high* loudly 67, 1602; festive 932, 1033; noble; *adv.* high; loudly
highlich adj. splendid
highly adv. highly, erect; in festive fashion 983; devoutly 755, 773
hightly adv. fitly
hille n. hill; *on hille* on any (castle) mound, anywhere
hir pron. her
hit pron. it
hitte v. hit; fall 427; befall 2511
ho pron. she
hode n. (1) hood
hode n. (2) order (of knighthood) 2297
hoghes n. hocks
holde n. stronghold 771; possession 1252
holde adv. loyally
holdely adv. loyally, carefully
holden past participle of holde hold; bound 1040; beholden 1828
hole adj. whole, intact; amended 2390
holly adv. wholly

holsumly adv. healthfully
holt(wode) n. wood
holw adj. hollow
Holy Hede, the Holywell 700 n
holyn n. holly
homere v. hammer, strike
hondele v. handle, take hold of
hone n. delay
hoo interj. stop! whoa!
hope v. think, believe; *hope of* hope for 2308
hore adj. hoar, grey
hose n. stockings
hostel n. dwelling, lodging
houve n. headdress
hove v. tarry, halt
hoves n. hoofs
hult n. hilt
hunte n. huntsman
hyde n. hide, skin
hye n. haste
hye v. hasten
hyght past tense of hete promise
hypp v. hop

ilk adj. same; *of that ilk* of the same (colour) 173, 1930
ilyche adj. alike, the same
inmyddes adv. in the middle; *prep.* in the middle of
innermore adv. comparative further in
innogh adj. and adv. enough; plenty
innowe plural of innogh enough
inore adj. comparative inner
inwith adv. and prep. within
irk v. (impersonal) irk; *with him irked the burnes* the men were tired of
    him
iwis adv. indeed, certainly

jolily adv. gallantly
joly adj. gay
Jon St John the Apostle; *saynt Jones day* 27 December
jopardy n. jeopardy, peril
joyfnes n. youth
juel n. jewel, treasure

jugge v. judge, appoint
juste v. joust

kanel n. neck
kay adj. left
kene adj. bold
kenet n. small hound
kenly adv. boldly; bitterly 2001
kenne v. teach; commit 2067
kepe v. keep; be anxious to 546, 2142; await 1312; *kepe with carp* engage in conversation; *kepe the* take care 372
kerchofes n. kerchiefs
kerre n. marshy thicket
kest past tense of cast 1147
kever v. recover 1755; receive 1221, 1254; afford 1539; succeed 750, etc.; make one's way 2221
knage v. fasten
knape n. fellow
knarre n. crag
knit v. knot, tie, make fast
knokled adj. knobby
knorned adj. craggy
knot n. knot; *in a knot* in a cluster 1431
knowe v. know; acknowledge, recognize 357, 937
koyntyse n. skill
kyd past participle made known; known; famous; acted 2340; *kyd him cortaysly* shown him courtesy 775
kyn n. kind; *fele kyn* many kinds of; *all kynnes* of every kind
kynde n. kindred; *worldes kynde* human race; nature 321, 2380; *by kynde* as is fitting 1348
kynde adj. natural, seemly
kyndely adv. duly
kyrf n. blow
kyrtel n. kirtle, gown
kyth n. land, country

lace n. cord, belt
lach v. *(past tense and past participle laght)* take, get; catch hold of; draw 156
lachet n. latchet
lad past tense and past participle of lede lead
laft past tense of leve leave

laght *past tense and past participle of lach* take

lagmon *n.* (?) *by lagmon* in a string, strung out behind

lakke *v.* find fault with 1250; *yow lakked* there was lacking in you 2366

lance *v.* gallop

lante *v. past tense* gave

lappe *n.* flap, fold

lappe *v.* wrap

large *adj.* wide, broad

largesse *n.* great size 1627; generosity 2381

lasse *adj. and adv. comparative* less; smaller

lassen *v.* lessen

lathe *v.* invite

launde *n.* glade, field

lause *v.* loosen; release; utter 1212, 1766, 2124

lausyng *n.* loosening

lawe *n.* (1) mound, knoll

lawe *n.* (2) law; fashion 790

lay *v.* lay; utter 1480; *layd him biside* turned aside, parried 1777

layk *n.* sport, festivity

layke *v.* play, amuse oneself

layne *v.* conceal; cover up for 2124, 2128

layt *n.* lightning

layt *v.* seek; seek to know 355

lede *n.* (1) man, knight

lede *n.* (2) people, company 833, 1113, 1124

lede *v.* lead; have 1927, 2058; pursue 1894

ledeles *adj.* without company (without a squire)

lee *n.* shelter; castle

lef *adj.* dear, delightful

lege *adj.* liege, sovereign

leke *past tense of louke* lock

lel *adj.* loyal, true

lelly *adv.* loyally, faithfully

leme *v.* gleam, shine

lemman *n.* mistress

lende *v.* arrive 1675; go 971; take one's place 1002; dwell, stay 1100, 1499, 2440; *is lent on* is occupied with 1319

leng *v.* stay

lenger *adj. comparative* longer

lenkthe *n.* length; *on lenkthe* for a long time 232, far away 1231

lent *past tense and past participle of lende*

lentoun n. Lent
lere n. (1) cheek, face
lere n. (2) something worthless 1109
lere n. (3) ligature 1334
lern v. learn; teach 1878
lese v. lose
lest adj. superlative smallest 355, 591
let v. let, allow; cause to 1084; utter 1086; behave 1206, 1634;
let as (lyke) behave as if; *let be* cease from 1840; *let one* leave alone,
let be 2118
lethe v. make humble
lether n. skin
lette v. hinder; dissuade
lettrure n. lore, doctrine
leve n. leave; permission to depart
leve v. (1) allow 98
leve v. (2) *(past tense laft)* leave; give up 369
leve v. (3) live 1035, 1544
leve v. (4) believe, trust 1784, 2128, 2421
lever adj. comparative dearer; *that lever were* who would rather
levest adj. superlative most delightful
lewed adj. ignorant
lewty n. fidelity
lif n. life; person 1780
liflode n. food
light v. dismount; fall, come down
like v. please; like; *(impersonal) him likes,* etc. it pleases him
list n. joy
lithernes n. ferocity
littel adj. little; *a littel* some way away 2146, 2171
live oblique case of lif life; *(up)on live* alive, on earth
lode n. leading; *on lode* in tow 969; *in his lode* with him on his
journey 1284
lodly adv. offensively 1772; *let lodly* behaved with horror, professed
horror 1634
loft n. upper room; *(up)on loft* aloft
loghe past tense of laghe laugh
Logres England
loke n. look, glance
loke v. look, glance; protect 2239
loken past participle of louke lock
lome n. tool

longe v. belong to, appertain to

longynge n. grief

lopen past participle of lepe leap

lore n. learning; *with lore* learned

los n. renown

lote n. sound, noise, speech

lothe n. injury 2507; *withouten lothe* ungrudged 127

lothe adj. hateful; *thoght lothe* were loath 1578

louke v. lock, fasten, shut

loupe n. (1) loop 591

loupe n. (2) loop-hole, window 792

loute v. (past tense lutte) bend, bow; defer to 248; come down (from an upper room) 833, 933

lovely adj. gracious, fine; *adv.* graciously; in a friendly manner 981

lovelyly adv. graciously, amiably

lovie v. love

lowande present participle shining; brilliant

lowe adj. low; *on lowe* down (from chamber to hall) 1373

lowe v. praise; *to lowe* praiseworthy 1399

lowly adv. humbly

luf n. love, affection, friendliness

luf-lace n. love-lace, belt given as love-token

lufsum adj. lovely

lur n. loss, sorrow

lurke v. lie at ease, doze; *lay lurked* lay low 1195

lutte past tense of loute

lyft n. heavens

lyft adj. left

lyft v. (past tense and past participle lyft) raise; build

lyght adj. gay, cheerful; active, energetic; swift 199; *set at lyght* think little of 1250

lyghtes n. lights (i.e. lungs)

lyghtly adj. bright

lyghtly adv. easily, swiftly

lyk v. taste 968

lykkerwys adj. desirable, delicious

lymp v. befall

lynde n. tree (linden)

lyndes n. loins

lynde-wode n. wood

lyne n. linen; *under lyne* in linen (tag) 1814

lyre n. flesh; coat 2050

lyst v. (*impersonal*) please; *the lyst* it pleases you, etc.
lyste v. listen to; *lyste his lif* hear his confession
lystily adv. craftily; skilfully
lyte n. *on lyte* in delay 2303; *on lyte drowen* drew back 1463
lyte adj. little, few
lythen v. hear

madde v. act madly
Mador de la Port Mador the Doorkeeper
maghtyly adv. powerfully
male n. bag
malt v. *past tense* melted
maner n. custom; kind; manner
manse v. threaten
marre v. destroy
mas *3rd person singular present tense of make*
mate adj. daunted, overcome
mawgref prep. despite; *mawgref his hed* despite all he could do
may n. woman
mayn adj. great, strong
mayster n. lord; master
maystryes n. magic powers
me pron. 'ethic dative' 1905 see note
Meghelmas Michaelmas, 29 September
mele v. speak
melle n. *in melle* in the midst
melle v. mingle
melly n. contest, battle
menge v. mingle
mensk n. courtesy, honour
mensk adj. honoured
menske v. adorn
menskful adj. noble, worthy
menskly adv. courteously, worthily
menyng n. understanding
merci in *grant merci* many thanks
mere n. appointed place
mere adj. noble
merk n. appointed place
merkke v. aim at
mery aaj. merry, gay, fine
meschaunce n. disaster

meschef n. harm

messe n. buffet 999; food 1004; *messes* dishes 999

messewhyle n. Mass time

mesure n. measure; *mesure high* height

mete n. food; meal

mete adj. equal; *mete to* extending to

metely adv. fittingly

methles adj. immoderate, pitiless

meve v. move; arouse; set out 1965; *meve to* attack 1157, come to 1197

meyny n. household

mislike v. displease; *impersonal* 2307

mist-hakel n. mist-cloak

misy n. bog

mo adj. and adv. more

mode n. mind

moght past tense of may 872 (elsewhere *myght*)

molaynes n. studs at the end of a horse's bit

molde n. earth

mon n. man

mon v. 3rd person singular present tense must 1811, 2354

mone n. (1) moon

mone n. (2) complaint 737

more adj. comparative more; bigger

Morgne la Faye Morgan le Fay

morn n. morning; next day

moroun n. in *good moroun* good morning

mot v. (past tense most) may, must

mote n. (1) moat; castle

mote n. (2) moot, long single note on hunting horn 1141, 1364

mote n. (3) whit 2209

mounture n. mount, horse

mournyng n. sorrow

mowe plural present tense of may 1397

much adj. much; big 182, 2336

muchwhat n. many things

muckel n. size

mug v. drizzle

mulne n. mill

muse v. (?) think i.e. live 2424

mute n. pack of hounds; hounds' cry

myddel-erde n. (middle) earth

myd-overunder n. in *while mydoverunder* until well on in the afternoon

mynde n. mind, memory; *gos not in mynde* seems unlikely

mynge v. draw attention to

mynne adj. less

mynne v. think, judge 141; think (of); exhort 982; *mynne upon* give one's mind to 1681

mynt n. blow aimed (but not delivered), feint

mynt v. (past participle, mynt) aim, prepare (a blow)

mysboden past participle mistreated

mysses n. faults

nad v. had not *(ne had)*

naf v. have not *(ne haf)*

naked adj. naked; *the naked* the exposed flesh 423, 2002

nakerys n. kettledrums

nakryn adj. of kettledrums

nare v. are not *(ne are)*

nas v. was not *(ne was)*

nauther adj., adv. and conj. neither

nay v. past tense said no, denied

nayt v. name, recite

ne adv. not; *conj.* nor

nede(s) adv. of necessity

negh adv. and prep. near

negh v. approach; touch 1836

neked n. little

nere adv. comparative nearer; nearly 729; *prep.* nearer to

neven v. name, mention

newes n. genitive in *what newes* whatever new thing

nif conj. if . . . not (from *ne . . . if*)

nikked v. past tense in *nikked him (with) nay* said no to him

nirt n. nick

nis v. is not *(ne is)*

nobelay n. nobleness

nobot conj. nothing but ('nobbut')

noke n. angle

nolde v. past tense would not *(ne wolde)*

nome, nomen past tense and past participle of nyme take

nones in *for the nones* for the nonce, indeed

note n. (1) affair 358, 420, 599, 1669

note n. (2) note 514

note adj. noted
noumbles n. numbles 1347 (see 1340–48.)
nowel n. Christmas
nowthe adv. now
nurne v. press 1771; offer 1823; call 2443; *nurne on* (?) perform 1669; *nurne hir ayaynes* (?) repulse her 1661
nurture n. good breeding
nye n. harm, trouble; *hit were nye* it would be hard 58
nye v. annoy, hurt
nyme v. take; *nyme by name for* designate 1347
nys adj. foolish

of adv. oft 773, 983, 1147, 1332, 1344, 1346, etc.
oghe v. (past tense aghte) possess; ought, owe it 1526
oght n. anything
olde adj. old; *for olde* because of age 1440
one adj. one; alone; *all (him, his) one* all alone; *him one* alone
ones adv. once; *at this ones* at this very moment 1090; *at ones* at one and the same time
onewe adv. anew
on-ferum adv. from a distance
on-stray adv. in a fresh direction
oquere adv. anywhere
or conj. than 1543
oritore n. oratory, chapel
orpedly adv. boldly
other adj. and pror. other; second 1020, 2350; *an other* otherwise 1268
otherwhyle adv. at other times
oute adv. far and wide 1511
outtrage adj. extraordinary
overclambe v. past tense climbed over
overtake v. (?) regain
overthwert prep. across (a line of)
overwalt past participle overthrown
overyede v. past tense passed over

palays n. palisade, fence
pane n. fur facing
papjaye n. parrot
papure n. paper
paraventure adv. by chance, perhaps
park n. enclosed game-preserve

passage n. journey
passe v. pass, cross, surpass
pater n. Pater Noster, 'Our Father . . .'
patroun n. lord
paumes n. flat ends of antlers
paunce n. armour for the stomach
paunches n. stomachs
paye v. please, satisfy 1379, 2341; pay 1941
payne v. in *him payne* exert himself 1042
payre v. be impaired, fail
payttrure n. breast-trappings of a horse
pelure n. fur
pendaunt n. pendant
pente v. have to do with
pertly adv. openly, in public
pervyng n. periwinkle
pese n. singular pea
piche v. attach 576; erect 768
pike v. polish
pine n. pain, grief; difficulty
pine v. reflexive take trouble
plate n. piece of plate armour
play v. amuse oneself
plede v. plead, press a claim
plyght n. strife 266; offence 2393
plytes n. hardships
polaynes n. armour for the knee
polyse v. polish, cleanse
porchas n. goods
poudre v. powder, sprinkle
poynt n. point; quality 654; good condition 2049; remark 902
poynte v. describe point by point
prayere n. meadow 768
prese v. press forward, hurry
prestly adv. promptly
preue adj. valiant
prevy adj. privy, discreet
prik v. spur, gallop
pris n. value, excellence; renown 1379; *your pris* your noble self 1247
pris adj. precious
prove v. prove, give proof of
prowes n. prowess

pryme n. early morning (between 6 and 9 a.m.)
prys n. horn call signifying the capture of the hunted animal
prysoun n. prisoner
pure adj. pure; noble; *adv.* entirely
pured past participle (of fur) trimmed to one colour 154, 1737;
    purified, refined 633, 912, 2393
purely adv. entirely, certainly
pyght past tense of piche pitch; pitched, struck 1456; was fixed 1734
pyked adj. spiked
pyn v. enclose 769
pysan n. neck-armour
pyth n. toughness

quaynt adj. finely made; skilful
quayntly adv. neatly, gracefully, skilfully
queldepoynte n. quilted covering
quelle v. quell, kill
queme adj. pleasing, fine
querry n. heap of game
quest n. baying of hounds 1150; *calle of a quest* give tongue 1421
quethe n. utterance
quik adj. lively, restive 177; alive 2109; *adv.* quickly
quit-clayme v. renounce claim to
quyssewes n. thigh-pieces, cuisses
quyte v. requite

race n. blow 2076; *on race* in a rush 1420
rach n. small hound
rad adj. afraid 251
rad adv. promptly 862
radly adv. promptly, quickly
raght past tense of reche reach
rak n. cloudbank
rake n. path
rande n. border, edge
rape v. reflexive hurry
rapely adv. quickly
rase v. (1) rush 1461
rase v. (2) snatch 1907
rasse n. ledge
ratheled past participle entwined

rawes n. hedgerows

rawthe n. a grievous thing

rayke v. come, go; depart 1076

rayle v. arrange, set

rechate v. sound the recheat (horn-call to gather the hounds together)

reche v. reach; offer, give; hand out 66

rechles adj. carefree

recorde v. repeat

recreaunt adj. recreant (i.e. confessing oneself defeated, cowardly)

rede v. (past tense redde) advise 363; manage 373; utter 443;
    direct 738, 2111

redily adv. without hesitation, willingly

redy adv. promptly

refourme v. recapitulate

rehayt v. encourage, urge on

reherse v. repeat, describe

rekenly adv. worthily 39; courteously 251, 821

rele v. roll; sway (in combat) 2246

remene v. recall

remorde v. recall with remorse

remue v. move, shake

renay v. refuse

renk n. man, knight

renne v. run

repayre v. be present

res n. rush

resayt n. receiving stations

resette n. habitation

resoun n. reason; speech 227, 392, 443; *by resoun* correctly 1344

restaye v. stop, turn back 1153; hold back 1672

restore v. restore; make restitution 2354

reve v. take away

reverence n. honour; *at the reverence* in (my) honour 2206

reverence v. salute

Reynarde the fox

rich adj. noble, splendid; *as n.* nobles 66, 362

riche v. direct 360, 1223; make one's way 8, 1898; prepare 599, 1130,
    1309, 1873, 2206; (?) draw tight 2177

richly adv. nobly; in a lordly way 308

right n. right, claim; justice 2346

rime v. in *rimed him* (?) drew himself up

roche n. rock

rocher n. rocky bank
rode n. rood, cross
roffe n. roof
rof-sore n. gash
rogh adj. rough
rokke v. rock; *rokked of* rubbed free of
rones n. brushwood
ronk adj. luxuriant
ronkled past participle wrinkled
rote n. (?) custom 2207
rote v. rot
roun v. whisper
rouncy n. horse
rous n. fame
rout n. jerk
rove past tense of ryve cut
roves n. roofs
ruche v. turn 303; make one's way 367
ruded past participle fiery red
rudeles n. curtains
ruful adj. grievous
runisch adj. (?) fierce, violent
runischly adv. (?) fiercely
rurd n. noise; voice
rusche v. make a rushing noise; *rusched on that rurd* went on with
that rushing noise 2219
ruthe v. bestir
ryal adj. royal
ryally adv. royally
ryalme n. realm
ryd v. relieve 364; separate 2246; *ryd of* strip off 1344
rygge n. back
ryght v. past tense in *ryght him* proceeded 308
ryme n. membrane
ryne v. touch
ryng n. ring; ring of mail 580, 2018; curtain ring 857
rys n. branch; *by rys* among the woods
rytte v. past tense cut
ryve adv. abundantly
ryve v. (past tense rove) cut

sabatouns n. steel shoes
sadly adv. firmly; sufficiently, long enough 2409
sale n. hall
salue v. greet
salure n. salt pot
same(n) adv. together
samen v. gather; come together 659
sanap n. cloth to protect table-cloth
saver adj. comparative safer
saverly adv. with relish; pleasantly
sawe n. words, utterance
sawse n. sauce
sayn v. bless with the sign of the cross
saynt n. girdle
scathe n. injury, disaster
schadde past tense of schede fall, sever
schaft n. shaft, handle, spear
schafte v. set, sink in the west
schalk n. man
schame v. be embarrassed 1189
schankes n. legs
schape v. (past tense schop, past participle schapen) fashion,
    contrive, appoint 2328, 2340; be arranged 1210
schaped past participle trimmed 1832
scharp adj. sharp; *as n.* sharp blade
schawe n. wood
schede v. (past tense, schadde) shed, fall; sever 425
schelde n. shield; tough skin on the shoulders of a boar 1456; slab of
    boar's flesh 1611, 1626
schende v. destroy
schene adj. bright; *as n.* bright blade
schere v. (past participle schorne) cut
schewe v. show, appear; look at 2036; produce 619, 2061
scho pron. she
scholes adj. shoeless
schop past tense of schape
schore n. shore, bank, hillside; *upon schore* aslant 2332
schote v. shoot; jerk 2318
schrof v. past tense shrove, confessed
schunt n. abrupt stop
schunt v. past tense drew back; flinched
schuve v. (past plural schoven) shove, thrust; press forward

schylde v. defend; *God schylde* God forbid

schynder v. sunder, break apart

schyre adj. bright, fair, white; *the schyre* the bright flesh 1331, 2256

schyrly adv. clean, without omission

scowt n. jutting rock

seche v. seek, go; *seche to* find one's way to 1052

segge n. man; *genitive* 574

sele n. good fortune, prosperity

sellokest adj. superlative most amazing

selly adj. wonderful, strange; *a selly* a wonder; *adv.* exceedingly

sellyly adv. exceedingly

selure n. canopy

selven n. self; *the burnes selven* the knight himself, etc.

semblaunt n. appearance; bearing, manner; demonstration (of regard), attentions 1658, 1843

sembly n. throng

seme n. seam (covered with ornamental strips of material)

seme adj. seemly

seme v. seem; beseem, be fitting 73, 679, 848, 1005, 1929

semely adv. becomingly, pleasantly

semly adj. fitting; fair

semlyly adv. becomingly

sendal n. silk

sene adj. visible, plain to see; open 341

sengel adj. alone

sere adj. various 124, 889; individual 1985; several 761, 822; *fele sere* many and various 2417; *adv.* in each case 632; *sere twyes* on two separate occasions 1522

serlepes adv. in turn

serve v. deserve 1380

servyce n. service; serving of a meal 130

sese v. (1) cease 1, 134, 2525

sese v. (2) seize, take

sesoun n. season, period, time

sete n. seat

sete adj. excellent 889

seten past tense and past participle of sitte sit

sette v. set; deliver (a blow); lay table 1651; establish 14, 625; *settes him* rushes 1589

settel n. seat

sever v. separate, cut open

sewe n. broth, stew

seye v. (past participle seyen) go, come
sey(en) past tense of se see
sidbordes n. side-tables, lower tables
siker adj. trusty; sure, certain 265; *adv.* certainly 1637
siker v. assure, pledge
sille n. floor; *on sille* in the hall
sister-sune n. nephew, sister's son
sithen adv. afterwards; *long sithen* long since; *conj.* after; since
skayne v. graze
skere adj. pure
skete adv. rapidly
skues n. clouds
skyfte v. shift, alternate
skylle n. reason; *by this skylle* (?) in this fashion 1296
skyrtes n. skirts; saddle-skirts 171, 601
slade n. valley
slake v. slacken, die away
slentyng n. slanting flight
sleye adj. skilfully made
sleyly adv. stealthily
slode past tense of slyde glide
slokes v. imperative (?) stop! enough!
slot n. hollow at the base of the throat
slyght n. skill, device
slyppe v. escape; slip
smal adj. small; slender 144; fine-textured 76
smartly adv. promptly
smeten past tense of smyte smite
smethely adv. smoothly, gently
smolt adj. gentle
smothely adv. deftly 407
smyte v. smite, strike; *smeten into* fell quickly into 1763
snart adv. bitterly
snaype v. sting, nip
sniter v. snow down
snyrt v. past tense nicked
soft adj. mild 510, 516
sojourne v. stay, lodge
solace n. pleasure, good cheer
somer n. the warm part of the year (including spring)
sone adv. at once, quickly, soon
sop n. morsel, snack

sore adj. painful
sorwe n. sorrow; imprecation 1721
soth adj. true; *as n.* truth; word of honour; *for sothe* truly
sothen past participle boiled
sothly adv. softly 673
sothly adv. truly
sounde in *all in sounde* in safety
sounder n. herd of wild pigs
soundyly adv. soundly
soure adj. unpleasant
sowme n. sum, quantity
space n. in *in space* soon, in due course
spare adj. restrained i.e. tactful
sparlyr n. calf of the leg
sparre v. spring
sparthe n. battle-axe
specialty n. partiality, affection
spede n. speed; success, achievement
spede v. speed; prosper; get done 2216
spedly adv. to good effect
spelle n. speech
spelle v. speak
spend v. past tense and past participle clung 158; fastened 587
spenne n. (?) hedge; *in spenne* there 1074
spenne-fote adv. with the feet together (in a standing jump)
sperre v. strike
spetos adj. cruel
spie v. spy, espy; inquire 901, 2093
sprenge v. spring; break 2009
sprent v. past tense leapt
sprit v. past tense sprang
spure v. ask
spyces n. spices, spiced delicacies
spyt n. harm
stable v. establish, fix
stablye n. ring of beaters
stad past participle set down 33; present 644; standing 2137
stafful adj. cram-full
stalk v. stalk; walk cautiously 237
stalle n. standing; *in stalle* erect
stalworth adj. stalwart
stange n. pole

starande present participle staring, glittering

start v. (past tense start) start, spring; flinch 1567, 2286

statut n. solemn agreement

stave n. club

stayn v. colour

stedde n. place

stek v. past tense clung

stel v. past tense stole, crept

stele n. handle 214, 2230

stele-bawe n. stirrup-iron

stele-gere n. steel-gear i.e. armour

stemme v. halt

steven n. (1) voice 242, 2336

steven n. (2) appointment; appointed day 2008

stif adj. strong, bold; stiff

stightel v. preside 104; deal with 2137; rule 2213; *stightel the upon* confine yourself to 2252

stille adj. motionless, quiet; *adv.* quietly; privately; humbly 2385

stilly adv. softly

stoffed past participle lined, padded

stoken past participle fixed 33, 2194; shut 782; crammed 494

stollen past participle stolen, stealthy

stonde v. stand; stand and take from 294, 2286

stor adj. severe, mighty

stounde n. time

stoune v. astonish

strakande present participle sounding the 'strake' on hunting horns 1364 n

straunge adj. strange; visiting (i.e. not a member of the household) 1028

strayne v. restrain, manage

strayt adj. tight-fitting

streght adj. straight

stroke past tense of strike strike, spring

strothe n. small wood

strye v. destroy

stryf n. resistance

strythe n. standing, stance

stubbe n. stock, stump

sture v. brandish

sturn adj. stern, forbidding, serious; *the sturn* the grim knight 214

stythly adv. stoutly

sue v. follow

sum adv. in part, somewhat 247

sumned past participle summoned

sumtyme adv. formerly

sumwhyle adv. sometimes; formerly 625

surfet n. transgression

surkot n. surcoat, gown

surquidry n. pride

sute n. suit; *of a sute, of folwande sute, in sute* to match; *of his horse
sute* to match his horse

swange n. waist

swap v. swap, exchange

sware adj. square

sware v. answer

swenge v. rush, hurry

swethle v. wrap

sweven n. dream

sweye v. rush down 1429; stoop down 1796

swoghe adj. dead (silence)

swyere n. squire

swynge v. rush

swyre n. neck

swythead v. quickly; vigorously

swythely adv. quickly

syde adj. long

sye past tense of se see

syfle v. reflexive blow

syke v. sigh

sykyng n. sigh

sylveren adj. silver

syn conj. and prep. since

synne adv. since then

sythe n. (1) time; case (i.e. group of five) 656; *by sythes* at various
times

sythe n. (2) scythe 2202

ta imperative singular of take

table n. table; projecting cornice 789

tache v. attach

take v. take; assign 1966; commit 2159; receive, experience 2448;
discover 2488, 2509

takles n. tackle, gear

tale n. speech; conversation; story; report
talenttyf adj. desirous
tan present tense plural of take take; *past participle* taken;
    circumstanced 1811
tapit n. tapestry; wall-hanging; carpet 568
tappe n. tap, knock
tars n. rich fabric from Tharsia
tary v. tarry, delay
tas imperative plural of take take; *tas to none ille* do not take it amiss
    1811; *3rd person singular present tense* takes 2305
tayles n. numbers, tally (with pun on *tails*) 1377
tayse v. pursue
tayt adj. merry; sturdy
tech n. spot, guilt
teche v. teach; direct; *teches him to* directs his attention to 1377
techles adj. spotless, irreproachable
telde n. dwelling
telde v. erect, set up
teme n. theme
tene n. trouble, strife
tene adj. rough; perilous
tene v. harass, torment; grieve 2501
tent n. intention; *in tent* intending
tent v. attend to (business)
terme n. term; appointed place 1069; appointed time 1671
tevelyng n. endeavour
thagh conj. though
thar v. need
thede n. country
then conj. than 24, 236, 333, 337, etc.
thenk v. (past tense thoght) think, intend
there adv. introducing wish 839
there conj. where 353, 694 etc.
theroute adv. out of it; out of doors 2000, 2481
thertylle adv. to it
thewes n. manners, behaviour
thider adv. thither
thik adj. thick; *adv.* densely, closely; hard 1770
think v. impersonal (past tense thoght) seem (to me etc.)
tho adj. plural those, the
thoght(en) past tense of thenk and think
thole v. allow; endure

thonk n. thanks
thore adv. there
thrast n. thrust
thrat past tense of threte threaten
thred n. thread; *negh the thred* near the limit
threpe n. insistence 1859; contest 2397
threpe v. contend
thresch v. thrash, strike
threte n. force, violence
threte v. threaten; attack 1713; press 1980
thrich n. rush
thrid adj. third
thro adj. steadfast 645; vigorous, festive 1021; fierce (ones) 1713;
    oppressive 1751; *adv.* vigorously 1867, 1946
throly adv. heartily
thronge past tense of thrynge press
throwe n. time
throwe v. (?) turn out 1680
throwen past participle of throwe throw; tied 194; well-knit 579;
    thrown 1740
thrye adv. thrice
thryght v. past tense thrust; pressed upon
thrynge v. press, make one's way
thrynne adj. third
thryvande adj. abundant
thryvandely adv. abundantly
thryven past participle fair
thulge v. be patient (with), yield (to)
thurgh prep. through, over; *thurgh all other thing(es)* beyond
    everything else 645, 1080
thurle v. pierce a hole in
thwarle adj. intricate
thwong n. thong
til prep. until; to 673, 1979
tite adv. quickly
titlere n. hound
to adv. too 165, 719, 1529, etc.
tofylch v. pull down
toght adj. stout
tohewe v. cut to pieces
token n. token, sign; teaching 1486; *tyteled token* inscribed title 1515
tokenyng n. indication

tolouse n. red fabric from Toulouse
tomorn adv. tomorrow morning
tone past participle of take
toppyng n. forelock
tor adj. difficult
torace v. pull down
toret past participle edged
tortor n. turtle-dove
torvayle n. hard task
tote v. peep
toun n. dwellings of men, court
tournay v. tourney, joust 41; double back 1707
towch n. touch; hint 1301; *plural* strains of music 120; terms of an agreement 1677
towen past participle journeyed
towrast adv. (?) awry
trammes n. schemes
trante v. dodge
trase v. set as an ornament
traunt n. practice
trauthe n. truth; fidelity, integrity 626, 2470; troth, pledged word 394, 403, etc.
travayl n. journey
travayle v. make a (wearisome) journey
traveres adv. in *a traveres* from side to side, across
trayle v. trail, follow
trayst adj. sure
treleted past participle latticed
tressour n. hair-net
trestes n. trestles
tried past participle famous 4; fine 77, 219
trifel n. trifle; casual remark 1301; ornamental detail 165, 960; *never bot trifel* only a very little 547
troched past participle pinnacled
trowe v. trow, believe; trust 2238
true n. truce
trueluf n. true love (modern 'courtly love'); *plural* true-love flowers 612
trusse v. pack
tryst v. trust, believe
tryster n. hunting station
trystyly adv. faithfully

tulk n. man
tuly n. red fabric; also *adj.*
turned past participle turbulent 22
tusches n. tusks
Tuskan Tuscany
twynne v. be separated
twynnen past participle (were) plaited
tyde n. time; *high tyde* festival
tyde v. befall, be due
tyffe v. prepare
tyght v. (past participle tyght) arrange; spread 568; hang 858;
   intend 2483
tyrve v. strip
tyteled past participle inscribed
tytle n. title, right 626; authority, evidence 480
tyxt n. text; *of tyxt* textural, authentic 1541

uch adj. each
uchone pron. each one
ugly adj. gruesome; threatening
umbe prep. round
umbe-clyppe v. encircle
umbe-folde v. enfold
umbe-kest v. cast (for a scent) round
umbe-lappe v. interlace with
umbe-teye v. past tense surrounded
umbe-torne adv. round
umbe-weve v. envelop
unbene adj. unpleasant
uncely adj. ill fated, (?)wicked
uncouple v. unleash
uncouthe adj. unknown, strange
undertake v. perceive
undo v. cut open
unethe adv. hardly
unhap n. mishap 438; misfortune 2511
unhardel v. unleash (hounds)
unlace v. cut up
unlewty n. faithlessness
unlouke v. unlock, open
unmete adj. monstrous
unrydely adv. in confusion

unsleye adj. unwary
unsoundyly adv. menacingly
unsparely adv. unsparingly
unspured past participle unasked, without asking
unthryvande adj. ignoble
untrauthe n. faithlessness
untyghtel n. unrestraint; *dalten untyghtel* revelled 1114
upbrayde past participle pulled up
uphalt past participle raised up, high
Uryn King Urien
urysoun n. strap attaching the helmet to the collar of the shirt of mail
Uter Uther Pendragon
utter adv. further out (into the open)

vayres n. truth
venge v. do vengeance
venquyst v. past tense was victorious in
ver n. spring
verayly adv. verily, assuredly
verdure n. greenness
vertuus adj. powerful 2027 n.
vewter n. keeper of greyhounds
vilanous adj. churlish
vilany n. conduct appropriate to villain or churl; vice 634, 2375;
    discourtesy 345
visage n. appearance
voyde v. vacate 345; purify 634; relieve 1518; *voyde out* clear out
vyage n. journey

wade v. wade, stand in water
wage n. pledge; *plural* wages
wake v. stay up late
wakkest adj. superlative weakest
wale adj. choice, excellent
wale v. choose 1276; *wale your won* choose your own course of
    action, do what you please 1238; look for 398
walke v. walk; spread 1521
wallande present participle welling up
walt v. toss
walt past tense of welde possess
walter v. roll, run
wan past tense of wynne win

wande n. staff 215; branch of a tree 1161
wane adj. lacking
wap n. blow
wappe v. rush
ware adj. aware; on guard; as hunting cry 1158
ware v. employ; deliver 2344
warely adv. warily; *wareloker* more cautiously 677
warp v. cast; utter; offer 2253; *warp on* don 2025
warth n. ford
waryst past participle cured, recovered
waste n. desolate place
wathe n. danger (also *wothe*)
Wawayn Gawayn (in lines alliterating on 'w')
wax v. *(past tense wex)* grow
wayke adj. weak
wayne v. bring; send 264, 2456, 2459; urge, challenge 984
wayte v. watch, look
wayth n. game (won in hunting)
wayve v. wave; *wayve up* throw open 1743; do (honour) 1032
we interj. ah!; *we loo* ah well!
wede n. garment; *high wede* armour
weder n. weather
weghe v. bring
wela adv. very
welde n. possession; *at your welde* at your bidding 837
welde v. wield; possess, take possession of; spend 485
wele n. wealth, joy; *for wele* because of its costliness 2037, 2432
wel-haled past participle well pulled up
welkyn n. sky
welnegh adv. almost, well nigh
wende n. turn
wende v. go, turn
wene v. *(past tense wende)* think, expect; *wene wel* know
wener adj. *comparative* more beautiful
Wenore Guenevere (in lines alliterating on 'w')
werbelande present participle whistling
werbles n. warbles, trills
were v. (1) wear
were v. (2) ward off 2015; defend 2041
werk n. work; *plural* deeds 1515, 2026; embroidery 164; designs
    216; workmanship 1817, 2432
werne v. refuse

wernyng n. resistance
werre n. war, fighting; manner of fighting 1628
werre v. fight
wesaunt n. oesophagus, weasand
wesche past tense of wasche wash
weterly adv. clearly
weve v. bring, give
wex past tense of wax grow
wharre v. whirr
whethen adv. whence
whether pron. which (of two) 1109
whether adv. nevertheless 203
whether adv. introducing direct question 2186
whette v. whet, sharpen; make a grinding noise 2203
whiderwarde adv. whither
while conj. while; until 1180, 1435; *prep.* until
whyle n. time, short time; *the whyle* for the time being 1791;
   the . . . whyle during 940, 985
whyssyn n. cushion
wight adj. lively, vigorous; *wightest* most valiant 261,
   swiftest flowing 1591
wightly adv. briskly
wil v. will, desire, wish
wille n. will, desire, good will
wit v. (present tense wot, past tense wyst, wysten) know
wlonk adj. noble, glorious, fine
wod past tense of wade
wodcraftes n. hunting skills
wode adj. mad
wodwos n. trolls of the woods
woghe n. grief, wrong 1550 n.
wombe n. stomach
won n. multitude 1269; course of action 1238
wonde v. hesitate, shrink
wonder n. marvel
wone n. dwelling-place
wone v. dwell, remain
wonnen past tense and past participle of wynne won
wont n. lack
wont v. (impersonal) lack
worch v. work, do
word n. word, reputation 1521

worme n. dragon
worre in *the worre* the worst of it
worschyp n. honour
worschyp v. honour
wort n. plant
worthe v. become (also *worthe to*); come to pass 485; fare 2096; come to 2134; *worthe as yow likes* let it be as you please 1302; *me schal worthe* it shall be done to me 1214; *me worthes the better* it will be the better with me 1035; *wel worthe the* may things go well with you 2127
worthily adj. worthy, noble 343
worthily adv. honourably; fittingly
worthy adv. courteously 1477
wot present tense of wit know
wothe n. danger
wowche v. vouch; *wowche hit saf* vouchsafe it
wowe n. wall
wowyng n. wooing
wrake n. distress
wrast adj. loud
wrast past participle turned, disposed
wrath v. anger, afflict; *impersonal* 1509
wreyande present participle abusing
wro n. nook
wroght(en) past tense and past participle of worch worked
wroth adj. angry, fierce
wroth v. past tense stretched himself (writhed)
wrothly adv. fiercely; *comparative* 2344
wruxled past participle wrapped, clad
wy interj. ah!
wye n. man, knight
wyf n. wife; woman 1001, 1495
wyght n. creature, person
wyke n. corner
wylde n. wild creature
wylede adj. skilful
wylle adj. devious 2084
wylnyng n. desire
wylsum adj. out-of-the-way
wylt past participle escaped
wynde v. wind, come round again
wynde-hole n. windpipe

wynne n. (1) joy
wynne n. (2) advantage, gain 2420
wynne adj. delightful, gratifying
wynne v. (past tense wan, wonnen; past participle wonnen) win;
  bring, conduct; come 461, 1365 etc.; make one's way 1569;
  wynne me find my way 402
wynnelych adj. pleasant
wyppe v. (1) wipe 2022
wyppe v. (2) whip, slash 2249
Wyrale Wirral (Cheshire)
wyrde n. fate
wysse v. guide
wyst(en) past tense of wit know
wysty adj. desolate
wyt n. reason, judgement, intelligence, cleverness; *plural* wits;
  fyve wyttes five senses
wyte v. look

yare adv. soon
yark v. ordain, set
yarrande present participle snarling
yate n. gate
yaule v. yowl
yayne v. meet, greet
ye n. (plural yen) eye
yede(n) v. past tense went
yederly adv. promptly
yef v. give
yelde v. (past tense and past participle yolden) yield, give, deliver,
  give back, recompense; *yolden him* allowed him passage through 820;
  reflexive surrender 1215, 1595
yelpyng n. vaunt, challenge
yen plural of ye eye
yep adj. fresh; valiant
yeply adv. promptly
yeres-yiftes n. New Year's gifts
yerne adv. eagerly; swiftly
yerne v. be eager, yearn 492, 1526
yette v. grant
yeye v. cry out
yirne v. run, pass
yode v. past tense went 1146

Yol *n.* Yule, Christmas
yolden *past tense and past participle of yelde* yield
yolwe *adj.* yellow, sallow
yomerly *adv.* piteously
yore *adv.* since long ago
yrn *n.* iron
Ywan Ywain

Zeferus Zephirus, the mild west wind which blows in spring